TURN & BURN

The Scriptwriter's Guide to Writing Better Screenplays Faster

CJ Walley

BENNION
KEARNY

ABOUT THE AUTHOR

CJ Walley's here for the gritty movies, the rebellious movies, those films that pack a punch far harder than their budgets would suggest. 2012 was the year he started screenwriting from Staffordshire, England, and it's been a hell of a ride, from his early scripts being featured by Amazon Studios to writing LA-based features *Break Even* starring Tasya Teles, James Callis, and Steve Guttenberg, *Double Threat* starring Danielle C. Ryan, Matthew Lawrence, and Dawn Olivieri, and *Night Train* starring Danielle C. Ryan, Diora Baird, Ivan Sergei, and Joe Lando, the last two of which he co-produced in partnership with multi Emmy-award winning filmmaker Shane Stanley, executive producer of the #1 Box Office hit *Gridiron Gang* for SONY Pictures starring Dwayne "The Rock" Johnson.

CJ's all about the craft and all about the love. It doesn't matter to him if it's Tarantino or *Twilight*; he always looks for the good in everything. As a huge fan of American New Wave films of the 70s and a child of the Independent Cinema Movement of the 90s, his big dream is to make cult films that showcase strong female characters in the truest sense of the term – strong in character – with the rebellious tone and gritty aesthetic of those eras. This is something he's in the process of doing through his production company Rebelle Rouser.

He's also here to help change the industry, too, in any way he can and for the better. In 2016, frustrated by the costs and cliques that screenwriters and filmmakers face when trying to share or source material, he built and launched the free script hosting website Script Revolution, which has flourished into a thriving community consisting of over 11,000 screenwriters and industry members.

For more information, visit www.cjwalley.com

DEDICATION

To John for convincing me my ideas weren't terrible.

To Matt for telling me to revaluate my life and start writing.

To Rob and Sammi for getting through my early efforts.

To RB and Amanda for providing a place to grow.

To Sandra for first turning my words into reality.

To Shane for giving me my big break.

To Paul for always keeping me grounded

To Neil for showing me the coolest places in Hollywood.

To Lee for being a wise mentor in the land of make-believe.

To Joey for sticking with this struggle for as long as you could.

To James for having to proofread and edit my dyslexic ramblings.

To my mum, dad, sister, and family for never giving me anything
but unconditional support since day one of setting off on this
crazy adventure.

THE BOOK

This book is what Bob Ross would call a "happy accident". It started as a collection of notes I made after becoming frustrated with giving repeated advice over and over again in various online screenwriting communities. Nobody was really having the realistic conversations we needed to have about craft development, artistry, and career-building, while the same basic questions cycled around on a near-weekly basis. Those notes quickly became pages and those pages formed a very basic and quick to digest online guide that covered the bare essentials on screenwriting along with the story development process I'd refined over many years.

While that guide helped many new writers, it was never really enough, and I knew it was never really enough. I had a lot more to share, and it was sitting on a bench next to a canal sipping coffee and talking all things automotive and cinematic with fellow writer, filmmaker, and publisher James Lumsden-Cook that an opportunity arose to finally address the issue.

So, here's the result, a book I never really intended to write but which very much needed to be written. A book I hope feels a lot less like a get rich quick scheme or a set of formatting rules and more like an honest and practical guide to chasing what is the very lofty dream of getting paid to make things up, write them down, and have famous people act them out in front of cameras, preferably with a few car chases in there for good measure.

I hope it brings some sense to all the madness.

CJ

TABLE OF CONTENTS

FOREWORD

Firstly, before I get into things, I want to talk a little about who I am and my motivation for sharing my thinking on screenwriting. When I wrote parts of this guide, I was a nobody – five years into writing – with no real success stories to speak of, other than a lot of short script options that never seemed to manifest into production. I'm pleased to say that, since then, at this time of writing – another five years later – after getting the green-light and travelling from the middle of England to sunny California to be on set and meet some of my heroes, I've become a working writer-producer who's written and helped produce three independent feature films, the kind of films that get released and distributed internationally via major platforms and covered by the likes of Deadline, US Weekly, and KTLA Morning News.

While you may not find the movies I'm involved with playing in your local theatre or pictures of myself on the red carpet, I am building a very real screenwriting career, and I feel that's important because it shows that the methodology I detail in this book works, and has been working for me for a long time.

I get paid to write movies now, the dream has been realised, and I love my new career dearly. It is, quite frankly, a wonderful way to work and live. I want you to have this experience for yourself because it is indeed life-changing and incredibly fulfilling, even at an indie filmmaking level. But I need you to know this, too; I tried to give up writing multiple times, and the slog of trying to break in to the film industry is still very fresh in my mind. I've laid awake, night after night, worrying things would never happen. I've been reduced to tears by cruel feedback, which told me I didn't have what it takes. I've felt constantly tormented by the need to write while watching my finances run dry, my relationships wane, and my sanity deteriorate. I'm in the rare position where I have a foot in both camps and can relate to writers on both sides.

Something I've come to accept is that we do not choose to write, writing chooses us, and it's a heavy burden to carry in a world that has become reluctant to fund unknown artistic ambition. As a result, those of us who are chosen only have two paths we can realistically take... to try and starve the beast, or learn to tame it. The former, the choice to try and stop writing, will only lead to guilt and later regret. The latter, the choice to hone our craft and embrace our voice, can only lead to finding our love for it and, subsequently, the audience we desire. We have to invest effort to see a reward, but it's essential that effort is directed studiously toward becoming a better, more entertaining, more emotionally stimulating, more philosophically inspiring writer rather than simply exhausting ourselves with sheer output and hoping for the best. There is a creative genius inside you – that's why you're here, and many others aren't – but that genius must be humbled by learning before it becomes empowered with knowledge. To keep churning out material with the belief we have everything it takes and nothing more to discover within the craft, the art, or ourselves is the equivalent of clinging desperately onto the bull and believing it will tire before we do.

\ The artist is nothing without the gift, /
but the gift is nothing without the work.
Emile Zola

In this guide, I'm not trying to position myself as a guru in any way. I want to share my process and thinking for one simple reason, I know the struggle, and I'm sick of how that struggle is continually preyed upon by opportunists. I'm tired of how that struggle is exacerbated by endless subjective debates that seemingly make any commitment within the craft a crossroads between fame and fortune or pain and despair. I'm heartbroken by how that struggle is made so much unnecessarily more agonising than it needs to be that it causes so many keen artists to eventually doubt themselves and give up on their dreams. I want you to be a happy writer because there's every chance the art you go on to create may one day bring unexpected joy to my life. I also really don't want you to be an unhappy writer either because I've been there myself and know the anguish it can ultimately bring.

For what it's worth, I actually come back to this guide and reference it often, both to utilise its thinking and to remind me of its principles. What I'm sharing here, with you, is something I still get a lot of value from as a working writer. It is a methodology that makes the process easier for me while also generating better results. My hope is that it does the same for you. If you have any foreboding feelings going into this, please leave them at the door now and relax. This isn't about making your writing life tougher or beating you up. This is me reaching out my hand, with a smile on my face, and offering to help you up the mountain with a little less weight on your shoulders.

In the time a very much cut-back version of this guide has been available online, I'm pleased to say that I've been contacted by many who've found it useful and some that even described it as "game-changing" for their development. Knowing that it's working so well for people has inspired me to keep expanding upon it, resulting in the very book you're reading now, which has three times the content, along with stories from my own experience about gradually breaking in – warts and all.

That said, I accept there's a chance that some of the guidance I'm sharing may not be ideal for you. That leads me to open with the best piece of advice I can ever give another screenwriter: never trust a single source of opinion. Read, watch, and listen to the many information sources out there and reach a considered conclusion of your own, preferably the one that brings out *the best in you* as a writer. And remember, you absolutely do not have to pay to learn or to be discovered – I hope to demonstrate I'm proof of that, at least.

No Petty Rules, No Silly Formulas

As black and white as scripts may appear on the surface, screenwriting is a very subjective medium. I care about good craft and feel that comes from positivity, motivation, building on strengths, and tackling weaknesses. I also appreciate that, when we talk about "screenwriting", we are typically narrowing the art form down to western highly-commercial mainstream feature film writing. I'm not about to get into how many lines I believe an action paragraph should be, nor start claiming I've unlocked some sort of secret Hollywood template that guarantees success. What I'm sharing here is my processes and my mindset, which I believe maximise my creativity. The aim here, rather than being reductive and telling you what "not to do" (a phrase that shouldn't exist within the arts), is to instead build on the core of storytelling principles and artistic values that should empower you into knowing exactly what *you* need to do.

So Seriously, What the Hell is Turn & Burn?

Well, it's all about getting on with writing scripts as efficiently as possible. It's about asking ourselves the important questions which guide us while still encouraging us to put our fingers to the keyboard. It's a range of tools, methods, and thinking that I've developed that I've genuinely found useful. It encapsulates the creation and development of story from theme and premise to structure and scene. The focus is on pre-writing to help brainstorm ideas efficiently and maximise the entertainment factor without getting lost along the way and having to continually rewrite a complete script. It's also not too heavy as I don't want to go over the wealth of information that's already out there. It's aimed at writers who've found themselves in the position I did – feeling

I had a strong voice but struggling to get my head around the fundamentals of story mechanics and career building. The intent is to use Turn & Burn as a set of training wheels until the active practice becomes mostly subconscious second nature.

What it isn't is a shortcut. There are no shortcuts. There are plenty of bad turns, circular paths, and dead ends, though, and Turn & Burn is written to help avoid the many pitfalls you can fall into due to being given bad advice, preyed upon, or being sucked into self-destructive group-think. This all said (and please understand this before all else), finding your voice and honing your craft to the point of working within the film industry demands a tremendous amount of commitment in terms of time and energy. This is a pursuit that can take many years, even decades, to get even the slightest traction.

CHAPTER 1: CONCEPT BUILDING

Let's rewind to the beginning. Not the start of our stories, not the plot, not the structure, not even the format; let's go right back to what we believe about life. A bit of a heavy start, right? Maybe, but here's the thing, stories are tales about how life works – they are life-affirming. Storytelling is really the art of making things up to communicate a truth. Even if we aren't aware of it, deep down in our stories, there should be a theme that teaches the audience an important lesson about life, perhaps subtly, maybe via the protagonist's arc or through their actions. Regardless, it's there, and storytellers are able to provide the medicine that people need.

> It's theatre. It's an interpretation of life.
> It can be truer than life itself.
> **Valentine, *Clouds of Sils Maria***

Our theme is what we're really saying to the world through our story. It is our crisp and undiluted voice between the pages, and it's essential we identify what that theme is going to be *before* we start developing a new project. If you don't know what the theme is (sometimes referred to as the "message"), then here are some examples:

- *Romeo and Juliet* – Prohibiting the love of others due to petty tribal differences may cost the lives of our own children.
- *Bonnie and Clyde* – Embracing violent crime in the name of hedonism will inevitably lead to a violent demise in the name of justice.
- *Reservoir Dogs* – A ride-or-die friendship can exist between two people even when they are supposed to be sworn enemies.
- *Airplane!* – We can overcome even our deepest fears to save the day, providing we have the support we need around us.
- *Up* – Our willingness to go on adventures is often subject to having someone to share those adventures with.
- *The Lord of the Rings* – Sometimes, it's the most unlikely individual, or team of individuals, who are best suited to take on a seemingly impossible task.

Now, please understand that determining the theme from another author's work is often a case of interpretation. You may disagree with some of my off-the-cuff interpretations here, but the principle remains;

good stories are more than plot, they are a journey of discovery for the protagonist that we witness and learn from as a result. This is fundamentally what makes stories pleasurable to experience. They reassure, educate, and warn us about the trials and tribulations of life itself, and that's a form of philosophical guidance wrapped up in casual entertainment. Even at its most basic, a story about virtuous people beating a hostile force is still making the argument that good will always triumph over evil.

If you want to practise the art of deciphering theme from stories, you can do this quite easily to the point that it becomes instinctive. Simply take the end of the story and compare it to the beginning to find an arc.

- *Romeo and Juliet* – Two lovers from two feuding families commit suicide because they cannot stay together after falling in love.
- *Bonnie and Clyde* – An outlaw couple are gunned down by the law following an orgy of reckless violence.
- *Reservoir Dogs* – Two armed robbers, one an undercover cop, sacrifice themselves to protect one another after bonding during a heist.
- *Airplane!* – A passenger manages to safely land a plane in need of a pilot, despite boarding with no belief in themselves and a fear of flying.
- *Up* – An old man goes on the adventure of his life after his attempts to live an undisturbed existence crosses paths with an enthusiastic boy scout.
- *The Lord of the Rings* – A hobbit, along with an unlikely team, takes the One Ring to Mordor, despite being one of the smallest and meekest members of a fantasy world.

Some stories wear their theme on their sleeve, while others have it so buried that even the original writers need their fans to remind them what it is. Some of the most transparent examples tend to be American sitcoms where the cast will literally discuss what they've learned in an episode during its final image.

Getting a little pretentious for a second, art itself is the communication of profound truth, and thus the messages we want to communicate with the world tend to mean the most when they come from within. I say this because the easiest place to find the themes for our stories is via the lessons *we have learned for ourselves*. Look inward to your experiences and views on life to find not just inspiration but an urge to educate, reassure, or warn others.

As storytellers, it is our job to become masters of weaving themes so intricately within entertainment that consuming our thesis on life is both pleasurable and resounding. We are giving lectures in a way that's so engaging; the participants get goosebumps from the experience and live differently as a result. That's a lot of responsibility, right?

Seriously, though, profound stories teach us how to move through life and thus build the fabric of our cultural, moral structure. The stories we were told as children (religious or otherwise) were told to us with that greater goal in mind. These deeper messages form our society's moral affections, such as doing right over wrong, being dutiful, and showing respect.

Now, considering moral affections are one thing, being able to build on them is another. If only mankind had been expressing easily digestible yet profound statements related to moral affections, we could just reference at any time for inspiration... you know?... Like proverbs?... And if only someone had listed a big bunch of moral affections, categorised with inspiring proverbs, to help writers hammer home their theme all out of the kindness of his little black heart... like I've done in Appendix E of this book.

Example: In *Contact* (1997), the film revolves around the scientist Eleanor Arroway trying to communicate with aliens by securing funding and fighting to become the first human to be transported by a mysterious machine built from plans sent from the Vega star system. However, the story is really about the battle we all have between science and faith, particularly in the context of losing loved ones.

Hit the Flaw

By identifying the message behind the theme, we establish the lesson. However, what we have here is only the result, our thesis, our conclusion, our correct answer. Getting there is our journey, and our audience has to make that journey along with our protagonist. Our story is, in effect, proof of our theory. If people are willing to believe the events that unfold are plausible and satisfying, they are more likely and willing to believe the protagonist's resolve – along with what he or she comes to learn about life – through the process. Have you ever felt passionate about trying to change someone's mind on a topic? How often have you supported your argument by using yourself, and how you came to change your own mind as an example?

Therefore, since we end our story with a thesis, we start our story with an antithesis, a demonstration of flawed thinking on the part of our protagonist. This gives them something to overcome and forms their overall arc. They have a misconception about life that must be addressed before they can find peace.

> **Example:** In *Mad Max: Fury Road* (2015), while seeking redemption for her acts as an imperator to a ruthless dictator, Furiosa believes the answer is to travel to "the Green Place" she recalls from her childhood but comes to learn it has become a toxic swamp. Initially choosing to keep heading into the endless salt flats, she has to come to terms with the fact that she's been deluding herself to the point of madness, and her redemption must come from fixing the problems at home. Most people can relate to the flawed concept of believing that escaping their home town and moving to a fantastical place will help them escape their problems in life.

Finding our flaw isn't difficult, providing we know the theme. We can take those stories mentioned earlier and reverse engineer them as follows:

- *Romeo and Juliet* – Two people from two feuding families believe their love will be enough to stay together indefinitely.
- *Bonnie and Clyde* – A couple of outlaws believe going out on a criminal rampage will give them everything they need in life.
- *Reservoir Dogs* – Two members of a criminal operation, one posing as such, believe they can go into a heist without forming any kind of human bond.
- *Airplane!* – An ex-military fighter pilot swears he can never fly again or be a hero due to his trauma and associated drinking problem.
- *Up* – An old man who's become a hermit since his wife passed away believes all he wants or needs is a quiet life.
- *The Lord of the Rings* – A hobbit, who is in no way a typical warrior, doesn't believe he's strong enough to protect and carry a precious item into the darkest realms of his world.

Get Plotting, You Little Devil You

It's important to note here that we're far from done with concept building in this chapter. If your head is full of thematic messages, but you're struggling to see how they become stories, that's fine. You're unlikely to find a plot by identifying a theme alone because plot and theme are like yin and yang, two very different elements that are more powerful together than apart.

You are most likely very familiar with the concept of plot and have plenty of ideas that flow in this area. I do not need to explain plot to you, but I do want you to know that a remarkably clever plot isn't essential to writing a good story. You can have a very basic plot, or even a new take on an old plot, and still weave together a fantastic script. In fact, even when you've dreamt up the most seemingly original plot ever, you'll most likely be able to find something out there that's remarkably similar.

> **Example:** Both *Thelma & Louise* (1991) and *Smokey and the Bandit* (1997) are stories about pursuit, based around escapism, with the latter being via a fault of love and the former via struggling against a power. While their basic plot is very similar – running from the law in a car – their stories are completely different.

Complex plots that are created *for the sake* of being complex can come across as gimmicky, too. So can having a big surprise twist, especially if it feels forced. In many cases, historically revered films are full of plot holes that don't detract from the enjoyment at all because they are so rich in other areas.

> **Example:** It's become a running joke now that in *Raiders of the Lost Ark* (1981), Indiana Jones has no obvious effect on the plot despite being the main protagonist, while in the *Back to the Future* franchise (1985-1990), Marty falls foul of a multitude of time travel paradoxes, some more obvious than others. Thankfully, our screenplays aren't as catastrophically vulnerable as the Space-Time Continuum, even though it may feel as such sometimes.

Plot ideas can often inspire themes, and vice-versa, as you develop a story concept. This is why it's important to spend some time getting your ducks in a row before committing to a draft, rather than trying to extract meaning and maintain causality at a later date. Knowing your theme early on – much like establishing your protagonist's flaw – is going to make constructing your plot a lot easier, too, as you have some idea of what your character needs to experience on their journey of personal change. Your idea about a teenager who goes back in time and goes up against his parent's high school bully may cause you to think about how we tackle bullies in general, and create a protagonist who refuses to back down when taunted, even when it's against their own interests. This might inspire further scenes where that flaw is demonstrated until they eventually learn to turn the other cheek and walk away.

Again, we don't have to face a blank canvas here when it comes to inspiration; there are sources out there to help us. For me, one that works well is The Thirty-Six Dramatic Situations contained in the book of the same name. (They can be found summarised on Wikipedia.) Studying the situations identified will quickly cause you to realise that most stories fall within a few dozen typical plot devices. By using one or more of these situations, we can easily piece together the mechanics of anything from a short story to a multi-season TV series.

We're going to get into story structure in the next chapter, and I'm going to make it incredibly easy for you to put your concepts through a process that gives you the foundation you need for your story. So, don't worry too much about the detail of your plot just yet!

Can I Get a Happy Ending?

Given that it's our theme that needs to resound from our story, we don't necessarily need our protagonist to 'win' to get the lesson across. There can often be something a little sappy about neatly tied up happy endings, something that strikes us as disingenuous and not life-affirming at all. It could be said that winning, well, it's kinda for losers.

There are four kinds of ending:

1. **Happy** – The protagonist wins, and their flaw is overcome.
2. **Bittersweet** – The protagonist overcomes their flaw but loses.
3. **Cautionary** – The protagonist wins but fails to overcome their flaw.
4. **Tragic** – The protagonist fails to overcome their flaw and also loses.

Each is just as effective at communicating a theme, but do so in different ways. The protagonist winning is irrelevant, providing the theme has been communicated, because their actions have proven a lesson we believe to be true. There is no wrong choice, but our ending should match our intended tone and have some bearing on the stakes at hand. If the lesson we are teaching is a brutal one, it may require a brutal ending to hammer home its point.

Our chosen ending also defines the protagonist's character arc; they either go from flawed to enlightened, or from flawed to further in the dark. Again, there is no right or wrong, they are serving as an example, and their failure might be the jolt to the senses the audience needs to take notice.

Example: *Se7en* (1995) has possibly one of the harshest endings a hero could suffer when Detective Mills finds out what's in the box John Doe has delivered to their final location. He is told by Detective Somerset that seeking vengeance means that he'll lose overall, but Mills commits the final sin regardless, an act that feels emotionally right even if it's pragmatically wrong. By sacrificing his career, Mills ultimately convinces Somerset to stay in the fight to try to make the world a better place. Maintaining the tone of the film since the moment it opens, the ending of *Se7en*, much like life itself, is ugly and uncomfortable.

Personally, I like to come up with a rough version of each ending type for every story I write and then choose the one which I feel works best for the script. This is good practice should you ever have a producer/executive feel your ending is too sappy, or too much of a downer, and you need to provide an alternative.

Example: Continuing from a previous example, the bittersweet ending of *Thelma & Louise* (1991) works as a satisfying conclusion because it fits the narrative that those who find themselves trapped and incriminated by their situation often have to accept they have no way out other than suicide. An arguably more tragic ending would have been for the characters to turn themselves in, thinking their side of events would be believed only to face a lifetime of incarceration.

Much like *Se7en*, there is no happy way to wrap up a story like *Thelma & Louise* because of the theme it dares to explore and the position it puts its characters in. There is, however, a purging of emotion which itself feels therapeutic as these characters accept their fate. The audience doesn't shed a tear so much for Thelma or Louise as they decide to just "go" into the Grand Canyon; they shed a tear for themselves and everyone else who has ever found themselves in the same life situation and decided they have no other choice.

Feel the Love

Spoiler alert: people are obsessed with love. Okay, you knew that, but – seriously – survival via reproduction is the greatest force in life, and thus we are drawn to anything that relates to it in any form… good or bad. You're probably going to want some sort of love story within all of this, and there's nothing really more entertaining and goal-setting than that. It's a good idea to think about where you want to go and what sort of love story fits. In many cases, particularly in romcoms, the love story itself highlights the theme.

Example: In *Pretty Woman* (1990), Edward Lewis has become so dehumanised by the pursuit of money he has lost his capacity to love. Treating girlfriends as a commodity, he eventually meets his match, Vivian Ward, in the most unlikely of scenarios and, despite trying to maintain a purely transactional relationship, falls for her so deeply it changes his entire approach to how he does business.

What's critical is that the love story suggests a *challenge* and thus conflict, because conflict equals drama. Your protagonist simply falling in love with someone and walking away with them like a trophy at the end isn't likely to be enough to draw people in. Even the most unromantic movies still put obstacles in the way of love. There needs to be complexity, and you get to decide how prominent this is within your story.

Example: In *Die Hard* (1998), John McClane's marriage with his wife Holly is breaking down at the beginning of the story. When confiding, in private, with his closest ally Sgt Al Powell, the topic of past regrets comes up between them. McClane, believing he's not going to make it, asks Powell to contact Holly when it's all over and pass on that he loves her; something he needs her to know as he deeply regrets their last interaction being an argument.

Of course, you are not forced to include a love story. Many great stories don't, and instead focus on other types of human relationships instead.

Lock n' Load Your Logline

There's a good chance, with just a little research and thinking about the above, that we've got enough plot and theme to rough out our premise in the form of a logline. The earlier we do this during development, the better.

A logline is an ultra-condensed synopsis that explains the absolute basics of your script. The term's derived from the tiny explanations for shows and movies that used to be printed in TV guides.

Loglines are pretty much impossible to write when we don't have a grasp of our premise; but they're a veritable delight when we've got things in order, so don't be afraid. By locking one down at this stage, we can come back to it now and then, to make sure we're staying on track.

My tip for writing loglines is to simply open up a blank document and try to summarise the premise in around twenty-five to thirty-five words. I like to copy and paste my attempt over and over while making little tweaks to improve and condense it. Too much stress is put on the intricacies of wording loglines when *what really matters is the concept behind them*. A compelling idea will always make for a good logline and, while it's great to add some pizzazz, it's not essential. They are ultimately a business-to-business tool designed to help communicate concepts quickly between industry members.

It's important to remember that we don't need to summarise our entire story with character flaw(s), theme, and ending; we only need our premise and sometimes the stakes. It's also fine to give away any unexpected twist if it's core to the story.

Since I run a big script hosting website (Script Revolution) and screen every script listing that's submitted, I've seen over ten thousand loglines from amateur screenwriters over the past five years; and boy have I seen a lot of bad ones.

Bad loglines tend to come in three forms;

1. **Too boring** – The premise simply isn't compelling enough to warrant interest.
2. **Too complicated** – The premise is unclear, unrefined, or buried in convoluted detail.

13

3. **Too ambiguous** – The premise has been reduced to what reads like a poster tagline.

Here are the loglines, straight out of the development notes, for my last three produced feature films;

- *Break Even:* "Four hedonistic extreme sports fans try to outrun the law and the criminal underworld in the hope they can launder drug money they've found while sailing."
- *Double Threat:* "With ruthless mobsters on her tail, a precarious young woman with a split personality becomes entangled with a man on a pilgrimage across the country to scatter his brother's ashes."
- *Night Train:* "A single mom struggling to make ends meet as a Hollywood teamster evades capture by a ruthless FBI Agent while running black-market medical supplies in her legendary souped-up pickup truck."

As you can see, the protagonist(s) are introduced along with a need in the form of a goal, and a challenge in the form of an antagonistic force.

There is a lot of pressure on amateur writers to come up with ideas that are "high concept", which means having a premise that's so simple yet compelling to the general audience, it can be summarised in only a few words, a poster image, or even just a title, and still generate tremendous interest. High concept ideas will always be desirable as movies have to compete for attention to make profits, but we cannot force ourselves to dream up high concept ideas on demand. We have to accept the kind of storytellers we are, and many of us are drawn naturally towards smaller, more nuanced affairs.

Example: *Jurassic Park* (1993) is so high concept that the title itself gives away the basic premise. It's no surprise that the writer, Michael Crichton, tends to come up with high concept ideas for most of his stories, many of which revolve around genetic mutation, and another one of which, *Westworld* (1973), is also about a future theme park gone awry. Wes Anderson, on the other hand, with films like *Moonrise Kingdom* (2012) and *The Grand Budapest Hotel* (2014), tends to pen much smaller feeling concepts that focus on quirky characters. Both are incredibly successful in their fields.

Never beat yourself up for wanting to write small stories. The indie scene is always begging for character-driven films that can be made on a budget. On the same note, always consider how you may be able to elevate an existing concept so it can draw more people in.

Tackling Titles

It's hard not to become somewhat obsessive about naming our story as early as possible. Indeed, it can feel like the lack of a name is a huge roadblock, stopping progression. I encourage you to try to push this concern to the back of your mind for the time being. It's not worth wasting energy on at this stage. If you have a title you're excited about, by all means use it, but don't be afraid to use something temporary for the sake of referencing a project or naming a document. Your energy is best spent elsewhere.

Titles, much like naming a pet, are something that can be more reluctant to materialise in your mind the harder you try. It's best to move on with more pressing issues; tackle the title issue later, should your subconscious fail to deliver a eureka moment during writing.

You don't need an amazing title at a script stage anyway. Sure, a good title may help get a script noticed, but it's not critical at a production level. The final decision is one for the lead producers to make a call on before release. That said, it's wise to stay away from very commonly used titles such as "The Road", "Obsession", "Shadows", or "The Awakening", which are not only highly unimaginative but which also say next to nothing about the content. You need people to believe you can be original *before* they turn to page one of your script.

Consolidating the Concept

Hopefully, as a result of the above, you should have some basic elements in place for your project(s) that give some clear direction in terms of theme, the arc of your protagonist(s), the basic premise behind your plot, choices of ending, a working title, and a roughed-out logline that summarises your concept. Essentially, you have everything you need to start structuring a story. To help keep this in order, you can make use of the worksheet I've included with this chapter.

Something you might also want to do here is consider other elements such as:

- **The antagonistic force** – This is most likely going to boil down to a single villain who is behind everything. It's wise to think just as hard about your antagonist as you do your protagonist. Again, come back to the theme for inspiration here. Your antagonist represents the opposite of your core message and doesn't need to go through an arc.

- **A fundamental irony** – Irony is a powerful tool in entertainment, and there's a perverse truth in how life is often ironic in the way it plays out. It's good to identify and develop an ironic conflict between your protagonists and the premise. This typically manifests itself in the form of the most unlikely person having to become the hero.
- **Set the tone/genre** – Venturing into a new story can be like riffing on a guitar. You can go in unsure if you want to pluck at the strings or thrash out chords. Try to define the nature of what you're intending to write and stick by it. Go with the excitement and energy you feel at the start, with the intention to carry it through to the end.

Ultimately, make sure you are comfortable and highly motivated by the feeling of what you have at this stage; it's going to set the tone for the project's duration.

What we shouldn't do, at this stage, is jump in and start drafting. While we're in a very exciting place, we're also at a very delicate stage where great ideas can quickly devolve into the equivalent of development soup. What we have here are what I call 'Trailer Moments', small beats that suggest a brilliant story but don't yet connect all the dots or have any meat on the bone. If anything, we need to pause and reflect on what we have and let the abstract side of our mind flourish by taking only notes, before letting the methodical side come in and get everything in order.

Development soup is a term used in the industry to describe a project that's lost all direction due to too much input and too many rewrites, usually at the request of the studio. Objectively bad Hollywood movies are typically the victims of development soup, as are the countless scripts that fail to make it into production. While more akin to a case of *design by committee*, or *too many cooks*, an individual writer can still run into the same issues by failing to follow a logical process that builds on a solid foundation and keeps the core story intact.

Turn & Burn Concept Worksheet

WHAT LIFE AFFIRMING LESSON IS BEING TAUGHT?

WHAT PROVERB SUMS UP THIS LESSON?

WHAT WILL BE THE PROTAGONIST'S FLAW?

WHAT DRAMATIC SITUATION WILL THE PROTAGONIST BE IN?

WHAT ARE THE STAKES?

WHO IS FALLING IN LOVE AND HOW?

WHAT TYPE OF ENDING WILL THERE BE?

STORY SUMMARY:

My Mistakes in Concept Building

When I first got into fiction writing, at the now seemingly tender age of 32, I was all plot and action. My stories were about big events but lacked any real philosophical depth. My sensational action scenes, despite being praised by professional readers as comparable to those found in the Indiana Jones movies, failed to plaster over what was *a lack of story* in its truest sense. The characters I'd written, while interesting people, knew exactly what they wanted from page one, had life worked out, and their entire concern was simply physically beating the antagonistic force to get what they immediately needed. I was big concept in terms of universe, mid-concept in terms of plot, and small concept in terms of character.

I'd fallen into the trap of believing films were simple because, on the surface, they often appear as such. You have a hero, you have a villain, and usually the hero beats the villain to get something. I was world building when I should have been character building. I was finding the character through the story rather than through development and, while they did have flaws, they weren't flawed views on life itself. As a result, I was writing stories that lacked any kind of theme, or at least didn't explore the theme until the eleventh hour. I didn't just lack an antithesis in my final act; I lacked a thesis to even begin with. My stories were screaming at the top of their voice without really saying anything of any real meaning.

I was, like many new writers (and underdeveloped stalwarts), obsessed with the aesthetic, the universe, the surface level detail. How does this thing look and sound, not how does this thing make you think? Worse still, my lead characters weren't particularly likeable. They were sexy women shooting things and driving fast cars with zero charm and one-dimensional personalities. I was writing expensive productions with cheap values.

My first script began development as a fan-fiction sequel to *Mad Max 2* (1981), aka *The Road Warrior*. I spent months writing that thing; dreaming up the world, designing the vehicles, establishing the history leading up to the post-apocalyptic setting in excruciating detail and did it while completely failing to realise just what a deep and profound story *Mad Max 2* really was at its core. Here was a richly-layered film about a man struggling to hold onto his humanity in a world where people are turning into animals and there I was, much like those marauders in the wasteland, scavenging for what I thought I needed while taking little of real value.

There were no love stories in my early scripts either. Sure, there was infatuation, kissing, sex, and relationships, but there was no romance, no courting, no complications, or failings. People were surly sex objects and, when they eventually let someone in, trophies that came with the big win at the end.

My scripts were a blast to read because of the action, but they weren't satisfying to digest because they said so little about life – other than maybe that it's the good people who eventually triumph, but we all know that's a cliché that isn't always true.

I wrote multiple action-thrillers and action-comedies like this with varying degrees of success and personal fulfilment. Readers were left polarised. Sometimes I got lucky and tapped into something special, but it wasn't by design and I couldn't really tell you *why* it had happened. Black List readers hit me with both high and low scores. I couldn't get past the quarter-finals in competitions, yet Amazon Studios featured one of my scripts after picking it out of ten thousand others. It was all very confusing; one second, I seemed to have 'it', and the next I didn't.

I exhausted myself doing this over and over, shifting into the genres of fantasy and drama, until I hit a wall about three years later. Everything eventually accumulated in the biggest cliché concept possible at the time: a *Hunger Games*-style story about an unlikely young female protagonist leading a rebellion in a dystopian future.

Incidentally, *Fury Road* was released the same year, and everything came full circle. Here was a true modern-day retelling of Mad Max by established pros, and while it was all built around an almost comically simple plot, it had something profound to say about humanity, our relationships with each other, and our relationship with the planet.

I had been conflating high concept with high budget. I was fixated on the plot within the premise rather than the characters within the story, and it was leading me further and further away from the kind of writing I enjoyed. I finally crashed because I was no longer enjoying the process. It was the first time I'd given up on a script midway and was truly lost.

While I'd been trying to hone my craft as much as I could at this point, I threw myself into reading about storytelling more than ever until something eventually clicked. The essence of a great story isn't contained within a logline; the essence of a story is based on what it teaches us about life.

Example: *Jaws* has a great premise. The police chief of a small resort town, dependant on tourism, must protect beachgoers from a monstrous great white shark that's lurking in the waters. However, little of this really encapsulates what makes Jaws a great story — the police chief himself is afraid of the water, the town mayor refuses to close the beaches, and his only hope in keeping his community safe lies in teaming up with a dysfunctional rag-tag band of social outcasts. These social outcasts are individually fascinating people to experience because of their outlook on life and the backstories that have given them their mindsets. The beauty of *Jaws* is in the execution. It isn't a story about killing a shark; it's an uncomfortable demonstration of how people react to having to face their demons.

Modern-day blockbusters aren't without their layers either. Ask anyone familiar with the *Fast & Furious* franchise what those movies are about, and they'll likely answer "cars and family" because, while those releases may be packed with ludicrous amounts of action, they do have a heart that's been there since the first film. As writers, we have to acknowledge and appreciate this, regardless of our personal tastes. We have to be writing stories that are at least as meaningful as the "dumbest" weekend spectacle, and many amateurs aren't doing that.

This, of course, all comes back to the theme. That was where it all suddenly clicked together for me. I wasn't making the theme a priority in my concept development. Once I started thinking hard about the themes suggested by my ideas, everything changed. To do this, I spent a lot of time studying proverbs and attaching those life-affirming statements to the dozens of short script ideas I had at the time.

I stopped writing features, and I dedicated myself to writing short scripts as a sort of story development boot camp. No more bells and whistles to distract from the basics. I forced myself to write complete, meaningful stories over and over, with a page limit of just six to seven pages and the bare minimum of logistical needs. My characters had to go on a developmental journey in just five minutes and who they were was just as important as the plot at hand.

The more I practised, the more comfortable I became with the uncomfortable. Those elements I didn't understand before I started writing short scripts gradually became an indulgence. My fear of writing anything but happy endings diffused as I came to realise that even the most tragic of finales can be satisfying, providing they communicate a truth about life.

After an intense period of writing nothing but shorts, I returned to feature writing with newfound vigour, writing stories that were smaller than ever in terms of budgetary needs, and far less dependent on action, but significantly more profound and engaging. I was now writing character-driven stories and had found my sweet spot with high concept situations in relatively small worlds. I could now put two people in a locked, empty room and easily get ninety minutes of entertainment out of them.

Now people were reaching out with nothing but admiration, and filmmakers wanted to turn my words into reality. I wasn't scared and lost anymore; I was determined and knew exactly where I wanted to go.

And you know what? I'm still writing about sexy women shooting things and driving fast cars too. If anything, I've doubled down on where my voice and passion lies. Writing better stories doesn't mean writing arty or pretentious stories; it means writing highly authentic stories that come from the soul. I know what I like; I'm just doing a damn sight better job of doing it justice, now.

Today, when I'm putting together a treatment for my producing partners, I make sure to nail the theme and that's a cyclic process that runs alongside developing the plot. One fuels the other, and vice-versa, as I work on my ideas. The theme gives me the character arcs because I *know* what those characters need to discover on their journey, just like I needed to discover what storytelling really gives to the world before I could move on to my next act.

Now we have the barebones of a story taken care of, we can move on to developing the core structure that will form the framework of our character's journey from beginning to end.

*

You can download this chapter's *Concept Worksheet*
(and all the others in the book) from
BennionKearny.com/TB

CHAPTER 2: STORY STRUCTURE

Structure tends to generate a lot of heated debate among screenwriters and, in my opinion, a lot of that debate simply isn't warranted and distracts from the point at hand. I've read through lengthy rants by writers adamant that three acts are better than five acts, and equally passionate rants arguing vice versa. People often tend to support structures like sports teams, as if everything else is in opposition and they must be loyal fans. But here's the thing, the way I see it is all through cheeseburgers… seriously.

How would you go about describing a cheeseburger to someone who'd never seen one? Would you say it's meat between two buns with a slice of cheese? Three components. Would you say it goes bun, meat, cheese, onion, tomato, relish, bun, sesame seeds? Eight components? It really depends on where you draw the lines and the level of detail you want to go into! However, the basic concept of a cheeseburger always stays the same, with the delicious filling being packed within something that can be held in your hands. Contemporary western, commercially appealing storytelling is really no different. Everything comes back to what's known as the monomyth, and all those arguments out there are just options on how to cut it up and describe each section.

> The monomyth, often referred to as *"The Hero's Journey"*, is a narrative pattern identified by Joseph Campbell in his 1949 book *The Hero with a Thousand Faces*. Campbell, influenced by the analytical psychology of Carl Jung, was able to show a structure common in most mythological hero stories, which brought the concept into the zeitgeist. While Campbell wasn't the first to spot this trend, his analysis, which breaks everything down into *three main acts*, is easily the most widely known and frequently referenced.

When it comes to structure, the right one to follow is the one that motivates us to write. It's as simple as that. I have no grievance toward a writer who is excited to write because they've read *Save The Cat* and love Blake Snyder's controversial beat sheet. I have no issue with a writer who's always found comfort working with three acts because they believe a story should have a beginning, a middle, and an end. I respect any writer who swears by The Syd Field Paradigm because it's worked for so many others.

In fact, there are a huge number of story structures out there that I encourage any writer to browse through with an open mind. Finding the one that works for you will be like finding the right set of pillows for your bed, or the perfect shoes for your feet. You'll wonder how you ever managed to live comfortably before.

For me, structure was my Everest. I started off writing with a talent for natural-sounding dialogue and huge action scenes, but structure I couldn't understand. I thought it would be something I could never get my head around, but now it's something I've come to love. It was through a very painful learning process that I came up with the Turn & Burn structure; I wish I could go back in time and hand myself this methodology when I started. The next best thing I can do is hand it on to you.

Yearn, Turn, Burn, Learn, Earn

Five simple words to create an endless number of story opportunities. Five simple words that are easy to remember yet summarise the elements of the hero's journey. Five simple words we can quickly jot down and start building upon.

Yearn – The hero. We are introduced to the protagonist, a fascinating character who lives in a compelling world. There is just enough conflict in their life to cause them to yearn for something more, but this is balanced by a level of comfort, which is causing them to stay in stasis.

Turn – The call. A Tipping Point changes the balance of the world enough to start the drama and set a goal via either an event that affects the protagonist or an opportunity that's offered to them. This triggers the antagonistic force which the protagonist soon becomes aware of.

Burn – The tests. The protagonist enters a world of heightened antagonism, which brings out their strengths and weaknesses. The protagonist's decisions are seemingly set to re-address the balance, but the conflict builds to a climactic event which creates a Point of No Return.

Learn – The revelation. The protagonist cannot balance out the downward spiral of increased peril, and there's seemingly no route either to the goal or back to their original world. However, they hit a Point of Realisation (a truth about life), which changes their mindset and re-establishes a belief they can re-address the balance.

Earn – The leap. The protagonist confronts the antagonistic force and risks everything they have available, but winning turns out to be even harder than they thought. Regardless of whether they win or lose in the end, they reach a Point of Acceptance that proves the life truth they now believe in to be true. We, the audience, find this truth to be life-affirming.

Yes, it's really that simple. The protagonist yearns for something more until their life takes a turn which causes them to burn their bridges, and they have to learn a harsh lesson about life before earning their ending. For further clarity, here is the Turn & Burn structure overlaid with other structures to show where it's similar and where it's different.

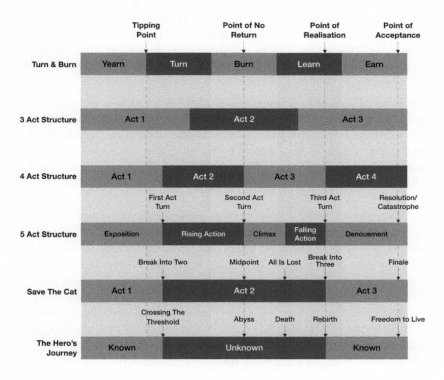

Let's go into a bit more detail.

Yearn

It's important your character is in stasis (somehow stuck in their life) because stasis equals death. As humans, we are designed to continually strive for change and, while we often try to seek out a perfect simple life that should never require much adjustment, it's well known that we'll soon adapt to the new normal and become uncomfortable.

It needs to be clear that your protagonist wants *more*; that want can be as shallow and superficial as you wish because the character is yet to become enlightened. They can be poor, rich, famous, homeless; none of it matters. Profound stories are messages about life that apply to everyone, and it can be powerful to dress them up in the most unlikely of characters.

Balancing comfort with conflict also means we can take even the most privileged of people and give them enough to worry about that they are uncomfortable and need to come to realise something important. We can contrast that realisation, too, by showing them actively operating in a manner that only serves to keep them in the dark.

> **Example:** In *Clueless* (1995), Cher Horowitz is a beautiful it-girl living at the top of the Beverly Hills socialite clique. She seemingly wants for nothing, even boasting a computerised wardrobe that can pick out the perfect outfit for her day, but in the words of her prodigy turned enemy Tai, Cher is a "virgin who can't drive". The former issue is a contentious one with Cher, who claims she is simply fussy, too mature for high school boys, and off the market anyway since she's saving herself for Luke Perry. What Cher fails to see is that, by becoming increasingly conceited and shallow in a bid to filter out the men around her, she's actually pushing away the kind of partner she really needs.

Turn

The tipping point that takes us into the next act can be as big or as small as we like. It can be innocuous on its own – like the straw that breaks the camel's back – or it can be of epic proportions and affects everyone in a life-changing way.

What really matters is that the protagonist enters a new world that's significantly different to their familiar one. This effectively makes them a fish out of water, regardless of the situation and setting. They could have everything they ever thought they wanted, or be watching their whole world fall apart – it doesn't matter as long as the journey away from normality has clearly started. There also needs to be a clear antagonistic force that may have been introduced in the previous act but is now actively engaging in conflict with our hero. The games have started. Done right, the audience should feel like all our intros and premise-setting are over, and now the rollercoaster has reached the top of the first climb.

Example: In *Gladiator* (2000), after leading his legions to victory across Europe, General Maximus Decimus Meridius is left with an impossible choice; go back to his family farm against the Emperor's dying wishes or become the reluctant successor of Rome in a bid to reinstate power to the Senate. A third choice is made for him when the traitorous Commodus, denied his place on the throne, tries and fails to have Maximus executed, leading the once-great general into exile as a Gladiator in North Africa. Despite still being a man of combat, Maximus enters a new world where he's a slave fighting for entertainment rather than purpose, and no longer has a family to live for.

Burn

Even if things seem to be going well on the surface, our protagonist needs to be headed on a downward spiral that is becoming impossible to escape from. The option to pull the eject lever and escape back to normality needs to be taken off the table, so there's only one direction the story can move – forward.

The Point of No Return can be an event or a decision, but it must be clear to the protagonist that they are now on this ride until the end, willingly or otherwise. This also reassures the audience that the story is only going to heighten the drama rather than diffuse it. It's also most likely that our antagonistic force is going to increase here either proactively, thus causing the Point of No Return, or reactively and thus exploiting the situation. What we are doing here is weakening our protagonist and proving that their current mindset is worsening their situation rather than fixing it.

Example: In *The Big Lebowski* (1998), Jeff "The Dude" Lebowski finds himself pulled into increasingly heightened peril, despite his indifference to any call-to-action other than reclaiming his stolen rug. He is drawn into dealing with kidnappers, attacked by marmot-wielding nihilists, double-crossed by his namesake over a small fortune, and used as an unwitting sperm donor by the woman he's fallen in love with. Despite The Dude's continued laissez-faire attitude on the surface, the damage it's doing to him spiritually finds a metaphor in the form of his 1973 Ford Gran Torino, which is crashed, stolen, used as a toilet, and ultimately set on fire.

Learn

The entire point of the previous act is to push our protagonist into their darkest moment, where they feel everything is lost and there is nothing they can do about it. Again, this is all relative. It doesn't matter if the stakes are losing a cheerleading tournament or an asteroid impacting the Earth, it is simply the biggest thing happening to the character in their life thus far, and all hope is lost.

What's essential here is connecting their flawed approach to life with their predicament, so it's clear to the audience that the protagonist is a victim of their own bad thinking, and needs to change their approach. The Point of Realisation, again much like the Tipping Point, can be subtle if needed or made very clear. The most common form is via a frank talk with an enlightened character who sees the protagonist's flaw and convinces them that they can become the person they need to be.

Example: In *Terminator 2: Judgment Day* (1991), Sarah Connor, who knows mankind is destined to create Skynet, an advanced artificial intelligence defence system run by the military that will inevitably become self-aware and deem all humans a threat, is haunted by vivid, recurring nightmares where she watches playing children burn to death in an atomic bomb strike over Los Angeles. When jolting awake from one of these dreams, Sarah sees that she's subconsciously carved the words "No fate" into a picnic table, causing her to realise the future is not set and, rather than continuing preparation for a nuclear apocalypse, she can take control and instigate a change in history before it happens.

Earn

Endings aren't about resolving the plot; they are about characters coming to terms with who they are and how that impacts their relationship with life. They typically find peace, even if it's peace with being a monster.

The real battle toward the end is earning that inner peace by proving – to themselves – who they can be. There is no more important a time for a protagonist to be active than in their final act. They have to be the ones pushing for a resolution even if they have help from all around them, and they need to look the antagonistic force in the eye with absolute conviction in their beliefs. They may be unsure if they are going to win or lose, but they know they are on the side of truth.

Without this conscious and deliberate leap of faith, you have a protagonist with unfinished business and, even if they win, it will feel like an empty victory. There is no external physical boon that can compensate for the inner spiritual need.

Example: In *Heat* (1995), Neil McCauley has a strict "thirty-second" discipline rule when it comes to attachments, believing a man in his line of work should never have anything in his life that he isn't prepared to walk out on if the cops close in. This theme is extended out to all characters central to the plot and accepted as true by all of them by the end. Michael Cheritto chooses to take part in the final heist and is killed, leaving behind a loving family. Trejo is left beaten half to death in his own home and pleading for a mercy killing when he's told his wife has been killed in the next room. Chris Shiherlis has to take one last look at his wife, Charlene, who refuses to identify him and allows him to flee forever. Donald Breedan, who is only involved with the gang for a few hours, dies almost immediately during the getaway, leaving his wife, Lillian, sobbing as she learns about it on TV. McCauley himself almost gets away with his new love, Eady, but due to his inherent nature, he creates a situation where he has to leave her behind without saying goodbye and thus proves his own rule true. Even Lt. Vincent Hanna, a detective with the best intentions, admits he cannot keep a marriage going and has a suicidal step-daughter due to the intense nature of his work chasing the likes of McCauley, something that they find mutual empathy in during their famous coffee shop scene. Incidentally, it's only Waingro, the story's villain, who's so psychopathic that he doesn't seek out true love, who eludes this emotional turmoil.

Story Structure Software

The story building tools within most screenwriting software packages aren't typically that great. If you are looking for something that will help you with story structure, allowing you to lay out a timeline and set key marker points in an organised fashion, then check out Prewrite (www.prewrite.com), which automates a lot of the process, makes things easy to manage, and includes the Turn & Burn structure along with others directly within its templates.

Old School Index Cards

Many writers like their writing to be as tangible as possible, and love the tactile feel of pens and paper. Index cards – the small 3x5 heavy card stock typically used in libraries – are a solid favourite for those who want to identify their scenes and physically move them around to get a feel for their story structure. Post-it Note-style sticky notes are a good alternative with the added bonus of being easy to use on a vertical surface, and most people can lay their hands on a ream of printer paper should nothing else be available.

Example: After *Reservoir Dogs* made a huge splash at Cannes in 1992, Tarantino, Roger Avary, and Stacey Sher (Tarantino's girlfriend at the time) travelled up to Amsterdam while discussing the development of Avary's script *Pandemonium Reigned*, a script Tarantino had bought from him about a boxer who – after refusing to take a fall during a fixed fight – has to try and evade the gangsters he's double-crossed while trying to reunite himself with a gold watch that's a family heirloom. Once in Amsterdam, and with Sher gone, Tarantino and Avery decided to pool all the best scenes they'd ever written, along with those they had for *Pandemonium Reigned*, and laid them out on the floor to see how they could fit together with Avary using his computer to combine them into sequences and thus (according to Avary at least), through a combination of both handwritten notes and digital technology, the basic storyline of *Pulp Fiction* was born.

Turn & Burn Story Structure Worksheet

YEARN

WHAT IS THE PROTAGONIST'S FLAW?

WHAT DOES THE PROTAGONIST DESIRE?

HOW IS THE PROTAGONIST'S LIFE COMPROMISED AND THUS BALANCED?

TURN

WHAT IS THE TIPPING POINT THAT CHANGES THE PROTAGONIST'S LIFE?

WHAT NEW WORLD DOES THE PROTAGONIST ENTER?

WHAT ANTAGONISTIC FORCE DOES THIS INTRODUCE?

BURN

HOW IS THE PROTAGONIST'S MAIN FLAW MAKING
THE SITUATION WORSE?

WHAT IS THE POINT OF NO RETURN THAT TRAPS THE
PROTAGONIST?

WHAT ARE THE STAKES AT THREAT FROM THE
ANTAGONISTIC FORCE?

LEARN

HOW DOES THE PROTAGONIST HIT ROCK BOTTOM?

WHAT IS THE POINT OF REALISATION THAT CHANGES
THE PROTAGONIST'S MINDSET?

WHAT IS THE PROTAGONIST'S NEW BELIEF SYSTEM?

EARN

HOW DOES THE PROTAGONIST PREPARE TO WIN?

WHAT IS THE PROTAGONIST RISKING TO WIN?

WHAT IS THE POINT OF ACCEPTANCE FOR THE PROTAGONIST?

My Mistakes in Story Structure

When I first started writing, I was writing in three acts, but I did not have a fully fleshed-out story structure. I established my world, I had an instigating incident that kicked off an exciting plot, and there was a big fight at the end. I was making a lot of it up as I went along. I couldn't work out why my stories were exciting and fun but failed to resonate.

I wrote this way because a lot of the advice out there told me I should write in three acts and, looking back, I have no quarrel with that statement on face value. The model of a beginning, middle, and an end is one that works for stories of all kinds, even motivational talks. The model could just as easily be interpreted as thesis, change, anti-thesis which, as per my thoughts on theme, sums up what stories tend to be. However, telling writers to structure a story in three acts – and simply leaving it at that – is a bit like telling a chef to serve an entree, main, and dessert. It's vague at best; no wonder I was struggling.

I also had a terrible, petulant animosity toward structure that held me back for too long. I fell into the trap of thinking art is pure expression and any form of academic thinking a creative hindrance. Given that everything I've learned as an adult has been self-taught, and I was a daydreamer at school, I don't have the best relationship with academia in general. Plus, as a huge fan of cinematic mavericks like Tony Scott,

Oliver Stone, and Quentin Tarantino, I simply couldn't believe these rebels ever subscribed to any rules, formulas, or templates. It also didn't help that writing forums were full of heated debates whenever the topic of story structure came up; some stating that it got in the way of telling the story you need to tell, even cheapening it, while others argued passionately that one structure model was vastly superior to another.

I'm going to make an uncomfortable admission. The often-maligned *Save the Cat* book by Blake Snyder saved me when it came to understanding the basic structure of *The Hero's Journey,* aka the monomyth. You see, I'm heavily dyslexic, and that comes with a bunch of associated learning issues where the mind really struggles to comprehend sequence-oriented processes. It was the *Save the Cat* beat sheet, as reductive as it may objectively be, along with Snyder's *Explain Like I'm Five* style explanations for each act, that I was able to lay over my first two screenplays and see the gaps.

The gap, or should I say gaping chasm the size of the Grand Canyon, that kept showing up was the section Synder calls Act 2B, the second half of the second act, which contains the Bad Guys Closing in, All is Lost, and Dark Night of the Soul moments. Despite having 120 pages of content per script, I was missing this core chapter in the protagonist's story and, as a result, a proper resolution and fully-formed character arcs along with it.

The thing is, it still took me another eighteen months of intense study and practice, along with another six feature scripts, until I truly got my head around structure and developed my own Turn & Burn system as a result. I read through so many books on craft and spent so much time reflecting. I became obsessed with trying to master this concept, which I initially thought I could never understand. Structure felt like such an abstract theory to me, and all the talk of character flaws, low points, and crossing thresholds just caused me to spiral into further confusion.

My attempts to write within a structure were small-minded too. I would make a protagonist's flaw something petty and fail to address the root cause behind it. In one of my stories, my protagonist had xylophobia – an irrational fear of woodland – as their flaw and their leap of faith was simply walking into a forest during the final act... not exactly profound, life-affirming, or even relatable if you're only scratching the surface. My structure points would be little more than a few beats lost within a lot of plot and distraction. Three acts also felt like a lot of empty space to fill and, even with copious development notes and treatments, I was still ad-libbing my way along a lot of the time.

That was until I eventually realised three important things:

1. Every story structure tends to be an interpretation of the monomyth.
2. The meat of the story is the protagonist's change from being in the dark to becoming enlightened.
3. Plot serves mainly as an excuse to demonstrate the theme.

Suddenly everything came into perspective. All those heated debates I'd seen online, adamant that one structure was better than another, were nonsense and misleading. I'd even read a book, a well-reviewed one too, that ranted for an entire chapter on why the five-act structure was the only one worth using. I'd been told that the *Save the Cat* beat sheet was *soooo formulaic* and that using it would stand out as amateurish. All of this was nonsense! It was people splitting hairs over something they didn't really understand. They were taking personal craft decisions and turning them into a team sport. There was a good reason these devout followers could take their structure of choice and fit the most revered stories in history into it – because how we tell stories, particularly heroes going on an adventure, is pretty much universal.

Now, rather than feeling like I had to pick a side and stick with it, I became empowered with the opportunity to take what I liked best about existing models and build on them until I had something that worked *best for me*. Finally, it was something that actually simplified things and gave my chaotic brain closure rather than anxiety.

Something I also came to accept was that well-structured storytelling is just ingrained into some people, and they use it instinctively even when they think they don't. I'm in no doubt that, had I been aware of the monomyth as a teenager, I would have seen it in every movie I'd watched for the next twenty years, and it would have given me a huge headstart when first I got into writing. Alas, I picked up on different things, which I'm sure gave me advantages in other areas early on. My big mistake was ignoring my weaknesses and hoping I could simply write my way out of them through sheer trial and error.

What really changed everything, though, was embracing the concept of building a story around a character. While I appreciate models like *The Hero's Journey* do focus on the protagonist's growth, they often present everything as a series of events and thus feel like plot. The Turn & Burn structure isn't about making a character go from point A to point B and experience X, Y, and Z. It's about having an overriding emotional attitude that shifts with each act and involves a few key points that indicate irreversible change for the protagonist.

The theme, as you'll know from the previous chapter, is a big player in terms of concept development but has little effect on the structure itself.

What I started doing better is using a system that pushed me to explore the theme and, the deeper I went, the more profound a message I discovered. This system also helped me to generate plot as a consequence because I now had a good idea of what my protagonist needed to go through to complete their journey. No more staring at a block of blank pages and thinking, *"What the hell's gonna fill this up?"*

Using structure, more importantly my Turn & Burn structure, has made things so much easier and faster. It has inspired so many new ideas in the early stages of development which I've been able to distil down to the best beats, moments, and sequences while giving just enough guidance that I haven't found myself lost and paranoid.

I've never felt restricted either, even when applying it to short scripts where a page may represent an entire act. I've only ever felt empowered and motivated. Plus, on top of all this, not only have my scripts been a lot easier to write, they're simply much better quality stories as a result.

Even now, as a working screenwriter with multiple produced features to my name, I still use this structure to develop all my projects, often turning synopses around lightning fast when I feel I have a great idea worth sharing. This is so powerful, in fact, that I once rapidly developed a concept in the morning, sent my producing partner a synopsis during lunch, and we had an offer of funding that afternoon. I will literally jot down the following and work outwards from there:

YEARN -

Tipping Point:

TURN -

BURN -

Point of No Return:

LEARN -

Point of Realisation:

EARN -

Point of Acceptance:

That two-page synopsis can then become a fleshed-out treatment, and that treatment the foundation of a script. It's a system that an image-based mind like mine can easily handle and, believe me, that's saying something when I can barely learn to tie a knot when shown over and over again, or add up the loose change in my pocket at the checkout.

There's a funny story in all this too. I mentioned *Mad Max 2* before, and I'll come back to it again. I grew up obsessed with this film and have a picture of Max Rockatansky's pursuit special on my bedroom wall. It always seemed like a dumb action movie to me with very little dialogue (not that there's anything wrong with any of that) and, while I knew it was basically a classic western with cars, I learned only recently (thanks to a documentary on its development) that George Miller was heavily inspired by *The Hero with a Thousand Faces* when he decided to make it.

Miller had gone through a tough time making the first Mad Max movie, which never felt like a complete story, but his new appreciation for the monomyth excited him to go back and face the monster. It was certainly reassuring to find out that one of my own heroes had gone through a similar journey in storytelling as myself.

Now you know the basics of what's going to happen in your story, and how your protagonist is going to grow throughout it, we can start to look at the people we need to surround them with to help make it all happen.

CHAPTER 3: CHARACTERS

Imagine you're playing an adventure game but, for some strange reason, there are no other sentient beings within that fictional universe, past or present. Would it even be possible to go on that adventure? Can a hero exist within a vacuum?

Character interactions are critical to guiding a protagonist through a story; they give motivation, guidance, and conflict. They are like the pop-bumpers in a pinball machine, pinging your hero around their world – seemingly at random – into situations both for better and worse.

> The context of character really includes every soul that impacts your story in some way. A dead relative who your hero lives by the advice of? That's still a character. A conscious creature that leads your protagonist in a certain direction? That's still a character. On the most part, though, a character will be a living human that falls into a tier of either lead, supporting, minor, or background.

Heroes

Assuming we have our theme and story all rounded out, and working on the basis that our characters are simply vehicles used to communicate our overall message via their actions, a lot of our work building the protagonist is already done for us. We know their key flaw, and we know how their ultimate ending dictates the direction of their character arc. We either prove our point through them winning or losing, or via they themselves realising or missing the lesson being taught. This is the beauty of building around story rather than character. We effectively set a clear compass direction and waypoints that – rather than restricting options – filter out the unnecessary, so we have the freedom to focus on what matters. Keeping things wide open isn't as good for our creativity as we might think. It's healthy to set off some triggers and define some boundaries. How you develop your hero beyond these core factors is up to you. They don't even have to be likeable; they just have to be relatable, and relatability comes from their values rather than their lifestyle.

Example: In *Payback* (1999), we're introduced to the anti-hero, Porter, stealing from a homeless busker, pick-pocketing a wallet, walking out on the bill for a meal, buying a firearm with someone else's ID, and kicking a door into the back of his wife. Despite all this, we soon warm to Porter as we learn how highly principled he is, and why he's behaving this way; he is a dangerous man betrayed over money. On top of this, Porter has a very dry wit that gives him a lot of great one-liners, preying to our fondness for a great sense of humour. The tagline for Payback was literally "Get ready to root for the bad guy", and Oscar-winning screenwriter Brian Helgeland manages to get us to do just that.

Villains

I'm a firm believer that a good villain is someone your audience would aspire to be if they weren't bound by morals. Antagonists aren't playing by life's rulebook, and there's something alluring about that. There's something deeper too. Your villain should be the hero of their own story. This is important and links back to the theme. Take the core of your life-affirming message and flip it – you now have your villain's outlook on life.

Remember, your life-affirming message is the profound truth your story demonstrates through the character arc of the protagonist. It's what they come to learn and harness to win.

By doing this, your antagonist is helping prove your message via contrast. Their wrong approach only helps to highlight your hero's growth into the correct approach. In a story about the importance of teamwork, your villain is an autocrat. In a story about how moral people win, your antagonist revels in immorality. In a story about how important it is to recognise love, your villain refuses to see it because they do not believe in it.

I say this because antagonists who are simply 'evil by nature' are poor clichés (often referred to in the business as "moustache twirlers") with only one dimension – doing bad. Again, your villain is the *hero of their own story*. Burn that into your mind. If you build them right, with a backstory that logically leads to their views on life, you should have a multi-faceted character who's refusing to address their flaws and change... thus bringing about their own downfall when facing your enlightened protagonist in the final act.

Example: Writer-director Martin McDonagh believes all characters, no matter how twisted, should hold life-affirming values, and he demonstrates this particularly well through Harry Waters, the ruthless London mobster and lead antagonist in his film *In Bruges* (2008). Harry has a strict moral code when it comes to operating within the criminal underworld, and the entire plot is about how his views on redemption negatively impact the protagonists Ken and Ray. One of his rules is that killing a child, accidentally or otherwise, is so unacceptable that the perpetrator should commit suicide on the spot out of disgrace. In the finale of the story, during the confusion of a pursuit through the city into a busy film set, Harry kills Ray by shooting him in the back but also unwittingly kills a dwarf wearing a school uniform in the process, causing him to believe he has shot a child. After reminding himself, "You've got to stick to your principles", Harry doesn't think twice, sticks his gun in his mouth, and pulls the trigger, thus proving that – while his moral code may be virtuous – his dogmatic view on atonement is ultimately short-sighted and self-destructive.

Everyone Else

Our other characters should be a product of the process and not there simply on a whim. If taking a character out of the story has zero impact on events, you have to ask yourself why they are there. That's another person to keep track of. Another name to remember. Another role to cast, costume, pamper, and feed. I once had someone share a script with me where the protagonist, a school student, was reprimanded by the principal and frog-marched to their office. As they passed a janitor mopping the floor, he was described in acute detail from his shoes to his sweater to his facial features and hairstyle. Was he a main character? No. Was he a supporting character? No. He was, in fact, a passing homage the writer wanted to include to Kurt Cobain. Nothing wrong with an Easter Egg like that, but save it for a conversation with wardrobe when you're making your movie.

When it comes to characters as a whole, we also have to ask ourselves what can be consolidated. Consolidation should always be on our minds with anything logistical as it keeps things as simple as possible. Can Person A and Person B be rolled into a new Person C who does everything the previous two needed to do? If so, seriously consider merging them.

The danger with supporting characters is them coming across as too similar to one another because you write them in your image. Even people within the most orderly of groups tend to differ wildly in temperament. It's something team-building exercises were designed to address. There's a quick and easy way you can push yourself to make sure your cast are varied in personality and bring a different dynamic to any interaction they have. In the Dungeons and Dragons world, they call it an Alignment Matrix, and it looks like this:

	Lawful	Neutral	Chaotic
Good	Lawful Good	Neutral Good	Chaotic Good
Neutral	Lawful Neutral	True Neutral	Chaotic Neutral
Evil	Lawful Evil	Neutral Evil	Chaotic Evil

What you are looking at here is a grid showing two spectrums and what they result in when they overlap. Your characters all fall somewhere between Lawful and Chaotic in terms of how haphazard their behaviour is, while they also fall somewhere between Good and Evil in terms of their moral fortitude.

You may have even heard other descriptions, including "chaotic neutral" (amongst others), based on a character's behaviour. This is where those terms come from. Remember what I was saying about adventure games and the need for characters to form a story? DnD is way ahead of us when it comes to building a universe. I like to try and make sure my supporting characters all place in different categories, ensuring a more multi-dimensional ensemble, and thus hopefully making things more entertaining.

Example: Ensemble movies tend to wear their alignment matrices on their sleeves, particularly those which are targeted at kids and want to teach them how every member of a team, never mind how quirky, is an essential asset. In *The Princess Bride* (1987), the highly unpredictable Westley is clearly Chaotic Good, while Buttercup and Fezzik, who tend to go with the flow, are Neutral Good. Inigo Montoya, however, the fencer on a moral crusade to avenge the death of his father, leans toward Lawful Good due to his strict principles and linear journey, all immortalised in his famous catchphrase "Hello. My name is Inigo Montoya. You killed my father. Prepare to die."

And Isn't It Ironic... Don't You Think?

When it comes to developing characters, I do think we can over-develop them in areas that don't really matter a great deal when it comes to creating a better story. Knowing an individual's birthday, religious belief, sexual orientation, and favourite band doesn't necessarily make them any more entertaining or believable unless those factors are highly relevant to their actions and, in turn, those actions drive the story where we need it to go. For me, I feel the best factor to introduce to any character is some sense of fundamental irony; teachers that bully, therapists that are neurotic, servants who manipulate, and so on. There's a feeling of truth within that. People often tend to be ironic in some way.

Example: In *American Psycho* (2000), Patrick Bateman leads a well-structured and clinically clean life where he has everything he could ever need: a cushy executive job with his own office, a stunning NYC apartment, and a high-status partner... all on top of the fact he is devastatingly handsome and charismatic.

The behind closed doors Patrick Bateman, however, is a chaotic serial-killing sexual deviant, obsessed with status, who's picking up streetwalkers in the shadiest areas of town in his stretched limo. Despite the well-cut suit, carefully trimmed haircut, designer glasses, and sophisticated business card, Patrick Bateman is an animal-like predator below the surface.

Know Your Character Hierarchy

I'm sure you have heard the terms *lead characters*, *supporting characters*, *minor characters*, and *extras* before, and imagine you know what those translate into in terms of time on screen and importance within the story. You should have some idea going into a project as to how prominent your characters are going to be, but also maintain a degree of flexibility as you dive into development. It's not unusual for supporting and minor characters to move up and down the hierarchy as you build the story, so don't worry if some roles grow while others shrink.

Example: On the surface, *Reservoir Dogs* (1993) has a flat hierarchy with eight criminals taking part in a jewellery store heist, six of them going by aliases named after colours, and one hostage who's a cop. However, the lead characters are Mr White, Mr Orange, and Mr Pink on the protagonist's side, with Mr Blonde, Nice Guy Eddie, and Joe Cabot on the antagonist's side. Mr Blue, Mr Brown, and Marvin Nash make up the supporting characters while the likes of Holdaway are minor characters.*

* I reserve the right to interpretation here and appreciate others may see this breakdown differently. I'm sure you get the point. Please don't send me hate mail.

Actor Bait

It's important you know *why* actors like to do their job, and I can assure you it's not because someone is writing down instructions on precisely how they should move and talk. Actors – good actors – are looking for exploration through character. They want to go through the experience of being another person in as much depth as possible, both for their own enjoyment and to do the character justice. Actors are looking for kindling that's on the brink of ignition point so they can be the flames that dance in the fire. It's our job to create that kindling in the form of rich, multi-faceted characters that they can study and ultimately become for the duration of a shoot (maybe longer). I don't say this lightly. I had a character once reference an author in a single line of dialogue, only for the actor who played them to tell me they were reading all of that author's works in their free time – and good for them. I'm sure they were getting a kick out of it. Just know how seriously dedicated actors take a role and allow that to motivate you further. Actors are unable to perform without writing. What we create is like oxygen to them. Be prepared for questions, too. Why is this character acting this way? What happened to them when we couldn't follow them between scenes? What's their entire life story up to this moment?

You know, a lot of people mock the infamous phrase *'What's my motivation?'* that so many actors request from their directors. But, really, a character's motivation at any point, just like our own, is backed up and built upon a lifetime of experiences which has formed them into the person they are (and with the views they have). In many ways, when we write, we are taking a first pass at acting out our character's actions based on nothing but the motivation we've created via our story structure. That feeling of exploration and reward that we go through needs to be passed on without being overly precious, and with open-minded interest in where the actor takes it. Ultimately, the script needs to be a gift to the production to build upon, not an instruction manual everyone must follow.

Example: In *The Fugitive* (1993), Dr Richard Kimble, an innocent man framed for the brutal murder of his wife, flees into the sluice of a dam in a desperate attempt to evade capture by the authorities but runs into what seems like a dead-end with Deputy Marshal Samuel Gerard right behind him, gun raised. It's at this point that Kimble and Gerard have their most famous exchange in the film, with Kimble shouting, "I didn't kill my wife!" and Gerard responding, "I don't care!" Interestingly enough, the response was changed at the request of Tommy Lee Jones from, "That isn't my problem." Both lines communicate the crux of Gerard's role and arc in the story well; his job is to bring fugitives in with no personal bias. This is what makes him so formidable; the fact he doesn't let his opinion on a fugitive's innocence or guilt get in the way of doggedly pursuing them. The changed version, however, besides sounding better, is much more personal and based on Gerard's perception of himself within the universe rather than his jurisdiction within an organisation. He genuinely does not care, and sees that as a strength when really it's a flaw.

The changed line worked so well at showing how much empathy Gerard lacks at the beginning of his arc compared to the end, and it's revisited during the final image of the film in the closing two lines where Gerard, now having captured Kimble, climbs into the back of the police cruiser with him and immediately removes Kimble's cuffs before handing him an ice pack to soothe his wrists. Kimble then quips, "I thought you didn't care," and Gerard replies sarcastically, "I don't. Don't tell anybody, okay?" as they are driven away into the night. Sometimes the best lines in a film may not be the writer's exact words but are borne out of the universe the writer has created.

The Power of Day Players

While it's easy to fantasise about our dream actors playing the leads in our stories, it's important to give the smaller roles a lot of love and attention. Obviously, this is simply better for the story. All characters should be as rich and multi-faceted as possible. However, there's another factor to consider here, which is more of a production issue; those smaller rolls are powerful bait for valuable day players (actors who come in only for a day or two during the shoot). Smaller projects have to make their budgets stretch to secure valuable talent, and day players can be some of the biggest gets. Established actors tend to love these roles, too, because they get to play characters outside their normal remit and have a lot of fun doing so in the process.

Some of my best days have been meeting day players and watching them work. On my first feature film, *Break Even*, we were lucky enough to attach Steve Guttenberg (*Three Men and a Baby*, *Police Academy*, *Short Circuit*) as an outlandish car collector turned weapons supplier who has three scenes in the movie. Steve is a childhood hero of mine and many others of my generation. He was the first person I met on a set that caused me to feel starstruck. He's also one of the first actors who told me he thought my writing was any good. As we stood there in the old Pimp my Ride workshop, surrounded by gleaming exotic supercars, Steve shook my hand tightly as we were introduced, looked me in the eye with a beaming smile, and said, "Great script, man! Love the pacing!" Watching Steve work, and sitting with him to talk about his process, was a real blessing, and it has also been the case with many other day players I've had the pleasure of meeting, too. So, make sure to do those smaller roles justice, as it may lead to some wonderful surprises.

Example: In *True Romance* (1993), three of the stand-out performances in the film are by Gary Oldman, Brad Pitt, and Christopher Walken, who play Drexl Spivey, Floyd, and Vincenzo Coccotti, respectively. Oldman got two scenes, Pitt got four, and Walken got one. While each actor could have easily shot their scenes in one day, their presence in the film is significant and iconic because they were given so much to work with in terms of character. In the case of Pitt, it's often said that it was this role, combined with a minor part in *Thelma & Louise* (1991), that helped him become a star.

Introducing Characters

The typical form for introducing characters is as follows:

CHARACTER NAME (age), description, continued action.

Far too much onus is put on the description side of things as writers try to create what feels like a form of haiku but somehow even more pretentious. A lot of fuss is made about how the character Teddy is introduced in the script for *Body Heat* (1981) by Lawrence Kasdan and is often shared around as:

"TEDDY, rock'n roll arsonist."

This actually isn't the full, original description from the script, so the promotion of it as an example is a little disingenuous. The full introduction is actually as follows;

"TEDDY LAURSEN, rock'n roll arsonist, is keeping the beat and mouthing the words along with the Bruce Springsteen tape on his workbench. Teddy is in his mid-twenties, dressed in a black T-shirt and jeans. His arson workshop is located in the basement of an old building. All around him are the tools and supplies of his trade: wire, rope, cans, vises, alarm clocks, chemical containers, and a huge assortment of mechanical implements. He keeps all his small accessories in dozens of cigar boxes, unlabelled. He knows where everything is."

Yeah, umm, that's a hell of a lot of detail, and it paints the Teddy character in a more artistic light when you're given the full description of both him and his operation. It is, however, unusually long – even in the context of the script in question – as no other character, including the main protagonist, gets introduced in anything close to this level of detail. The point I'm making here is that both the incorrect and correct quotation of this character introduction is a highly unusual example to work from. You can pick up pretty much any script for your favourite films and read a good, typical example.

Look, how you choose to introduce characters is up to you, and it doesn't matter how mechanical you need to be about it. You don't need to get clever here, as what matters far more is story. You don't need to assign anything physical such as attire, or define them in their initial actions or words either. Doing stuff like this is quite tacky and, if you try too hard, can cause a sudden shift in tone or pace as you try to impress the reader with content that barely has any effect on the quality of the script. Find your happy place here, and get comfortable with it. No actors are attaching themselves to a script based on a character description alone; there's no acting in that.

The place to get smart with character introductions is with the binding of descriptive length to importance, which can be a great way to communicate hierarchy to readers so they can quickly establish who they need to be paying attention to. The leads get a full name along with an age and description, while supporting characters get either a full name or short name – depending on their prominence – along with an age and no description. Bit-parts get a descriptive name only, such as ANGRY COP or NERDY KID. Note that the latter are gender-neutral to maximise casting choices and not default to any stereotypes.

> **Example:** Shamelessly embracing the camp of the grind-house aesthetic, the screenplay for *Planet Terror* (2007), written by Robert Rodriguez, introduces the main character, Cherry Darling, as follows: "Over titles, we are close on a pair of red go-go boots as the woman wearing them strides confidently onto the well-worn stage. This is CHERRY, a go-go dancer. She's too good at what she does, which means she should think about doing something else. Oddly, tears run down her face throughout the dance. Side note: The next time Cherry does this, people will die." It's worth noting that, as objectifying and exploitative as the genre often is, there is no mention of how attractive Cherry is or even looks. The focus is entirely on her competence, situation, emotion, and potential.

Killing Characters

It's pretty much inevitable, unless you plan to write Hallmark movies for the rest of your life, that you'll come to a time when you have to kill off a character. And when I mean kill off, I mean literally have them die in a scene. This can be a tough process to go through as a writer as you can easily become very much attached to characters, and death scenes can also be highly emotionally charged in terms of what's said during those final moments.

Here's my tip for death scenes.

If the death scene is to be brutal – such as in a horror or a thriller – and you are killing off a supporting protagonist, perhaps someone loved, write the scene as soon as you can. Even if it happens in the finale, get it written in all its shocking, horrific glory before you grow attached, as you are likely to show too much mercy otherwise.

If the death scene is to be beautiful, perhaps because it is a lover or elderly relative passing away, write the scene as late as possible. Make sure you have grown deeply attached to the characters to the point that their loss is as cutting *to you*, as it is to the fictional people around them. Try to share their pain and channel those raw emotions into those last breaths.

Something also worth noting is the impact that killing a character can have on a production, and that may change how you configure their demise. Before the shoot of my first movie, I got to meet up with the lead cast and was lucky enough to ride through Venice toward Marina del Rey with one of them in their classic Mustang. Over the rumble of the small-block V8, they turned to me and opened with, "I don't really die in this, right?" This caused me to realise that when an actor loves a role, they want it to continue for as long as possible. They want a sequel and they want to come back with everyone else. Plus, if the film performs well, the whole chain – from investors to production partners to sales agent to distributors to outlets – are going to want a sequel too, and god forbid you've killed off a much-loved character in a way that means they can never return. So, consider that.

Example: In the *Fast & Furious* franchise, they really pushed the envelope in terms of bringing characters back from the dead. Toward the end of *The Fast and the Furious: Tokyo Drift* (2006), Han Seoul-Oh has his Mazda RX-7 VeilSide Fortune t-boned at a junction, sending it tumbling down the road and pinning him within the crumpled wreckage as fuel pours over him. Before Sean Boswell can run to Han's aid, the wreckage quickly explodes in a huge fireball, strongly implying Han has been killed. Despite this, Han reappears momentarily within sequels and eventually in earnest as a main character once again in *F9: The Fast Saga* (2021), thanks to some highly inventive retelling of events to explain his survival. The plausibility of this explanation is contentious with fans, but ultimately the writers had to work with what they had — a death that seemed very much conclusive due to the way it had been written.

Turn & Burn Character
Development Worksheet

CHARACTER NAME

ALIGNMENT

DESCRIPTION

WHY IS THIS CHARACTER ENTERTAINING?

IRONY

My Mistakes with Characters

So, my first script had a male lead and, over forty scripts later, I've only once gone back and written another male-driven screenplay. It was pretty clear, even as I was writing my first story, that it was the females who really captured my imagination and emotional interest.

Something I came to accept very early on is that I love writing female characters. I'm compelled to. My imagination conjures up women when I dream up scenes. I care more when my protagonists are female. I feel more emotionally connected when writing about women. I don't know why this is, and I'm not quite sure I want to know why. As far as I'm concerned, it is what it is. Now, if you aren't already aware, I'm very much male – awkward.

Needless to say, having not lived my life as a woman and being at the mercy of my male gaze, I didn't do a great job at first. I didn't do my female characters justice. This is, in fact, a hard topic to write about because this (one of the things I care most about as an artist) may, for all I know, still be one of my biggest failings.

Thankfully, the feedback I get from the incredibly talented women who attach themselves to the roles in my produced scripts is overwhelmingly positive. If that wasn't the case, at least I'd have served as a poor example, not to follow.

I know for sure where I definitely went wrong in those early days, though. Firstly, I fell into the trap of treating men and women as completely different creatures and defaulting into tropes; the perfect mother, nagging wife, complaining girlfriend, saucy seductress, or broody spinster. I didn't write about the artist, engineer, protector, idealist, or executive who just so happens to be female. I didn't start with personality first and chose the best qualities and traits to make my story interesting. Instead, I figured, hey, this guy needs a wife/girlfriend/affair and fell back to the nag/bitch/sexpot that women are often projected as being.

Secondly, I completely misinterpreted the term *"strong female character"* as one that describes physical strength, defiance, and confidence. I forgot that perseverance, integrity, morality, loyalty, and leadership are tremendous strengths. I drew the conclusion that, just because my female characters kicked ass, they were strong. This led to me into writing one-dimensional female characters compensated by aggression; the Mary-Sue who chews her lip for ninety pages until she socks a jock in the mouth, the placid wife who suddenly finds a backbone and dresses someone down with a cutting rant, the exploitation girls that are as indestructible as they are sexy. This was uncreative writing that bred weak female characters lacking in depth or dimension. I forgot that characters are compelling to watch when they are complex, struggling, and broken – traits we can all associate with and love to watch others overcome.

The game-changer, though – the thing that changed everything – was the realisation that writing a character who doesn't share the same demographic as me isn't just about understanding how they behave within their world… but how their world behaves around them.

The fact is, women and minority groups of all kinds are treated differently in a multitude of ways I don't directly experience. When I take my car in for repairs, I'm typically approached in a different way to how a woman often would be. If I have to lead a business team in an assertive manner, I'm talked about in a different way to how a woman often would be. If I can't help but open up emotionally and cry within a group of my own gender, I'm most likely consoled in a different way to how a woman often would be.

The women I was writing, at first, held their heads up with unwavering confidence everywhere they went. They feared no one and needed no one. They commanded respect from everyone from the moment they met them and, of course, had no problem putting their romantic desires on the table, metaphorically or otherwise. I'm not suggesting women like this don't exist. I know a few that do. It was just remarkable how common they were in my writing.

As an action writer, I've always had a tendency to write female characters as tomboys. I used to think this was flattering but failed to appreciate that, while women don't have to be feminine, they also don't have to shed their femininity to fill the roles usually associated with male characters. I was writing men who looked like women and, in some extremes, women who were what we'd typically consider to be hyper-masculine. These included the woman who can beat up any man, the woman who knows more about cars and guns than the next guy (and isn't afraid to let him know it), and the woman who demands to lead and suffers no detractors. This was patronising and insulting. It was cringe-worthy, faux girl power. This wasn't writing women; it was playing GI Joe with Barbie dolls. Again, I'm not saying it doesn't exist out there, just saying it's uncommon.

Passive-aggressive action women rarely make good characters anyway; they often make unlikeable characters who are blatantly characterised to appeal to men, (and I'm not trying to make out women shouldn't be shown as enjoying typically male things either). I know many women reflect on their childhood and teenage years as showing tomboy tendencies, plus many women – while further embracing their femininity as they mature – pursue typically male careers and pastimes. I compensated for the issue with backstory; the girl who was brought up by her father, the woman trying to fill the shoes of her father, the girl trying to avenge her father. I eventually saw that women can be into the same stuff as men, but that's *not* criteria to be an action star, and it certainly doesn't need to define them as a person. It doesn't mean they need the mind of a man, it doesn't mean they need a contrived backstory, and it doesn't mean they need to be any less feminine.

I also saw that I was writing my women as sexual objects and not sexual beings. There's a fine line between female sexual liberation and male fantasy. A woman can indeed be an adventurous and highly sexual creature, of course, but the tendency seems to be to write femmes fatales and Bond Girl types where that quality defines their entire being (note that, in the latter case, it's always Bond Girl, never Bond Woman). We justify women offering unconditional sex as empowerment when it's sometimes just slutty behaviour born out of weakness. We labour sex scenes with a pornographic prose that leers on our female characters far too much. We don't ask ourselves often enough if two women are kissing for the pleasure of each other, or for every man in the audience. Sexpots aside, we men often write female character descriptions that are grossly objectifying. We linger on physical appearance from hair colour to high heels with no reason as to how it reflects character. Many times, I described a brunette with thick cascading hair and piercing green eyes because that's what I was fantasising about – I didn't stop to think if it was relevant. Not only was this poor writing, it was insulting to every female actor who doesn't fit those irrelevant descriptions. The same applies for age. We cast in bias of males, particularly when the character is over thirty, because that's when most women are somehow written off as attractive. The true factor in determining how attractive the character is will always be defined by character itself. By showing a shallow disregard for that, I was sending a signal to a lot of female actors to read no further.

So, I addressed this because I cared about growing as a person and doing a better job of what I love. I regularly read interviews by female actors, producers, and directors who brought a unique perspective to the table, often making it clear what they wanted to see in no uncertain terms. I made sure to take note of what female writers have to say on forums when the topic of strong female characters came up. But, mostly, I simply listened to the discussion, cared about what was said, and tried not to bury my head in the sand when facing uncomfortable truths. When you open your eyes to it, sexism is everywhere, every day, and it's sadly often in our scripts. Plus, and this may sound obvious, I talked to the women around me and listened to what they had to say.

Needless to say, this way of thinking didn't just revolutionise my female characters; it revolutionised *all my characters* because we're never really writing directly from our own experiences. We're always trying to get into the head of someone different to us, or facing experiences different to our own. The above applies universally. If we're going to do our characters justice, we have to understand how they've become the person they are, and yes, that also includes those we consider villainous.

I may be a very pulpy writer, but I'm very proud of the characters I write. I can't tell you how much it means to have the likes of Tasya Teles (*The 100*), Danielle C. Ryan (*The Cat in the Hat*), Joanna Pacula (*Tombstone*), Dawn Olivieri (*House of Lies*), Alisa Reyes (*All That*), Mary Mara (*Gridiron Gang*), Klea Scott (*Pretty Little Liars*), Arienne Mandi (*The L Word: Generation Q*), Diora Baird (*Wedding Crashers, Two and a Half Men, Cobra Kai*), and more decide to get out of bed in the morning and play a character I've dreamed up in my head. Well, I can tell you how much – it means the world.

Ultimately, I've learned to love listening to people when they tell me parts of their life story others think are boring. I love to ask questions so I can learn more about what they think and why they think it. I've yet to meet a person who isn't fascinating deep down and the plucky protagonist within their own story and, even if there is a lot of commonality between individuals, people never fail to surprise me with the unique challenges they've faced and overcome. It's through wanting to create remarkable characters that I've come to see how many unlikely heroes we're surrounded by every day.

So, now we have our concept, our basic structure, and our characters, it's time to start really making a scene.

*

You can download this chapter's *Development Worksheet*
(plus all the others in the book) from
BennionKearny.com/TB

CHAPTER 4: SCENE WRITING

By using the Turn & Burn story structure system, you should now be able to put together a very basic synopsis or at least a variation of one. This is something I advise practising as producing treatments – of all lengths – is a staple part of being a professional screenwriter. By completing a short synopsis of just a couple of pages (800-1,000 words), you are effectively writing out your story's pitch.

In fact, you want to really start honing your story development skills today! Take all your best ideas and write a short synopsis for each using one paragraph per Turn & Burn act (Year, Turn, Burn, Yearn, Earn). Hopefully, you'll find you have so much story there that you have to write each synopsis as efficiently as possible to fit within the word count. Through ongoing practice, you will also develop a natural ability to build stories out of ideas very fast.

That's the macro level story stuff covered, but we need to go down to a micro level before committing to actual drafting. You should know what you need to achieve through your scenes but not exactly how those scenes are going to play out.

While the story keeps us wanting, it's the scenes that keep us watching. If there's one area of screenwriting craft discussion that frustrates me, it's the lack of focus on scene structure. In fact, while I've seen screenwriters lose their minds over incorrectly formatted slug lines and other irrelevant superficialities, I've seen those same screenwriters discard any conversation about how to structure scenes as "overthinking things". This is the sad, and all too common, side of screenwriting, where so many obsess over the easy to understand and avoid the difficult to master.

The most common difference I notice between good writers and bad writers is the ability to write highly dramatic scenes that move the story, character development, and theme forward.

If you want actors to love you – and I sure hope you do – you need to give them scenes that take them on an explorative journey into another person's life; you need every day of shooting to be an adventure for them. Dedicated actors don't want to simply go through the motions of delivering tedious plot points, and nobody wants to sit through screen time watching them do that either.

The typical advice out there, when it comes to scene writing, is to enter a scene late and leave early. That's it. But that's not enough. That's not nearly enough! Maybe some other advice extends into suggesting there's always a turnaround, but again, that's pretty weak. Yes, scenes should be as lean as possible, and be dramatic, but we need more than that. What we need are the beats.

> Beats are the series of tiny moments that make up a story. Asking a question with intent is a beat. Being evasive with the answer due to guilt is a beat. Breaking down into tears with emotion is a beat. While some beats have much more impact than others, every single beat should matter and either be driving the scene forward, building the universe, or showing character change.
>
> Actors look for these beats in our writing when preparing for a scene and use them as emotional marker points in their performance. Editors identify them during cutting to make sure the pacing and focus are correct for the moment. Try to think of beats like the chords in a piece of music; they set the tone, they set the pacing, and everything else is built around them.

Good scene structure craft employs a process that helps us discover those beats. It gives us directions before we get lost deep in the emotion of the moment while drafting. Sort of like a sequential to-do list, we are laying out a basic choreography we can follow that keeps our scenes dynamic and meaningful.

We are effectively using the logical side of our brain now, with the intent to use the creative side later. This way, we avoid two potential pitfalls; entering a scene in a creative mindset but having no idea where to take it, and moving through a scene with such wayward creative giddiness that we lose track of the story we intended to tell.

Many new screenwriters wax lyrical about how their characters 'surprise' them with their behaviour as they draft. Personally, I don't see that as something to boast about. The process of creating art is overly romanticised by those who don't do it, and amateurs all too often try to re-frame their lack of discipline as being a true artist. I think that's making excuses to avoid the hard work.

While discovery is certainly part of the process, and a great line of dialogue can seemingly come out of nowhere, the beats of the story should be in place before the prose gets too flowery, much like how a painter knows their composition before they start mixing colours. They never really make it up as they go along – even if they do make it look natural.

Emotion Equals Entertainment

If there's one book I feel every screenwriter should buy or pester their local library to stock, it's Karl Iglesias' *Writing For Emotional Impact*. I know I'm not the only working writer who feels this way.

There's really no substitute to reading the book itself, but to summarise its message, we find emotion compelling, be it via poetry, novels, or movies. There is no substitute for it. Good stories are packed with emotion, and poor stories are starved of it. As screenwriters, it's our job to work out how to bring the most amount of emotion to a scene in every form possible, be it happiness, amusement, fascination, excitement, anger, fear, or sadness.

We are incredibly emotional beings, and stories allow us to experience the emotions we need to feel by living vicariously within a fictional world. There's a good reason why millions of us settle down in front of our TVs each evening and soak up daily soap opera episodes like our lives depend on it.

The catalyst for emotional entertainment is *conflict* and it's something that needs to be rife within our writing on multiple levels, including the internal (psychological) and the external (physical and personal). Comfort should only ever be fleeting, and scenes where there's no conflict at all should be reserved for the final images of happy endings. Conflict also doesn't mean the characters are necessarily unhappy or angry. They can be very positive but also up against a challenge such as a rapidly approaching deadline.

Example: The opening scenes of *Silver Linings Playbook* (2012) are chirpy, upbeat, and optimistic, but almost every moment is accompanied by some sort of conflict. When we open on Pat Solitano talking to himself in a mental institution, his rallying pep-talk is interrupted by a staff member knocking on his door and demanding he come out before we focus on the prison cell-like clinical mediocrity of his dorm. We then follow Pat being forced to take medication and spitting it out in secret, talking about negativity being a poison during a circle meeting, and being unexpectedly interrupted by his imposing mother during exercise. Despite his mother signing Pat out of care, the focus is on how bad an idea that is – to the jingle of high-security door keys and harshly-worded legal forms being signed and witnessed. The sequence ends with a highly comedic moment where Pat has his mother pick up his wacky friend,

Danny, on their way out of the car lot, complete with a towering box van pulling up behind and honking at them to move.

While our heroes and the characters around them are battling against the odds, our villains don't get to escape this either. They must also live in a world of constant conflict, and this is why some of the funniest scenes in movies, even in very serious ones, tend to be the ones where the antagonist is trying to go about their business while surrounded by a hapless team of idiots who don't seem to be able to complete even the most basic of tasks.

Puzzles

When it comes to scenes, the biggest trap new writers fall into is focusing on logistics due to the misconception they exist purely to serve the plot.

Logistics are the mechanics behind your script that allow the story to unfold, such as characters travelling to a certain location or an event that triggers additional drama. If you want a hero to be in a tower block when it's hijacked by terrorists, you have a logistical need to set up how the hero comes to be there, and how the terrorists execute their plan.

They have the characters explain/debate what they're going to do next while commenting on and explaining everything around them. This is known as *exposition* and it's best minimised to avoid scripts that read like workplace instruction manuals. It is tedious and all too often plays out like the writer feels the need to justify everything that happens in their story. In many ways, good scenes do the complete opposite of this and serve as an entertaining diversion from working through the logistics. Very little is actually explained in good movies and a lot simply plays out because the characters are following routine or already know what needs to be done.

Example: In the early scenes of *Pulp Fiction* (1994), we ride along with Vincent Vega and Jules Winnfield, two hit-men on their way to recover a briefcase on behalf of their crime-lord boss, Marsellus Wallace, that's currently in the hands of a group of amateurish crooks who've tried to double-cross him. Vincent and Jules are due to be there a little after seven-twenty-two in the morning, where they will be facing what could potentially be five armed and dangerous individuals, one of whom is an insider. However, even after fourteen pages of riveting scene writing, this is all we know about the logistics at hand, and we only glean it from snippets of dialogue and action. The focus instead is on the cultural differences between Los Angeles and Amsterdam, how protective their boss is over his wife, Mia (of whom Vincent is set to take out and entertain later), and their differing opinions on the sexual nature of foot massages. Through this, however – woven into the entertainment – is the setting up of two characters on very different arcs, the identification of a villain, the foreshadowing of a major plot twist, and the establishment of a precious object.

People love puzzles and will easily fill in the gaps themselves or wait patiently for things to fit together in time, even as they reflect on the movie after the credits have rolled or better understand it with repeat viewings. They are in it for the character drama, which provides the bulk of the entertainment while logistical needs take place around it.

Your audience doesn't need their hands holding all the way through but, if you are writing a summer blockbuster movie with a convoluted plot and fast pace that needs to play to a very wide audience (i.e., appeal the lowest common denominator), you can always add a catch-up scene now and then where a character will literally ask the others something like, "So, why are we here again?" and another character will give a quick summary of their current plan and the stakes if they fail to succeed. That said, the big action movies still try to keep exposition to a minimum.

Example: In *Aliens* (1986), we ride along with Ellen Ripley as she joins a Colonial Marines squadron sent in to the planetoid LV-426 to locate the colony of terraformers creating an atmosphere to make the air breathable. As they drop to the surface from the Sulaco deep space warship and make their way into the complex, we're given next-to-no-details on what the squadron intends to do, and how they intend to do it. Instead, we are constantly playing catch-up based on snippets like "Watch your corners!" and "Don't bunch together!" as they move deeper inside. We are just as confused, scared, and fascinated as they are.

The beats of these scenes are more focused on the Marines' reaction to the alien infestation (which we feel through them) and the ongoing power dynamic between Ripley and Lieutenant Gorman, where she points out the squadron is too close to the heat exchangers to use live rounds before having to jump in and take control when Gorman folds under pressure during a fire-fight.

A Nice Big Bowl of PASTO

In my opinion, there's no better place to look for good scene craft than playwriting because, in theatre, there's no hiding behind sensation, creative camera angles, and clever editing.

PASTO first appeared in the book *Primer of Playwriting* by Kenneth MacGowan back in 1951, but it is still taught as part of many MFA playwriting programs today. A twist on classical Aristotelian analysis, PASTO is actually structural theory for writing an entire play but works perfectly (maybe even better) as a micro-structure for scenes. On a very basic level, the characters go in with some kind of intent, face an unforeseen challenge, and exit with a new objective which sets up the intent for their next scene. What this creates is causality – every scene exists because the previous one set it up.

PASTO stands for: Preparation, Attack, Struggle, Turnaround, Outcome. It's all about how things flow in terms of what characters want to happen, how they try to make it happen, and how they have to deal with the results.

- **Preparation** – The characters go into the scene with a plan to achieve something.
- **Action** – The characters interact, and the conflict unfolds.
- **Struggle** – The drama heightens as the characters' actions increase the conflict.
- **Turnaround** – Something significant and surprising happens as a result of the drama.
- **Outcome** – The characters are now burdened with tackling the new issue.

Now, I think the first reaction screenwriters have when they look at PASTO is, "Holy crap! That's a lot to try and cram in a movie scene!" and it potentially could be, but that's the wrong way of looking at it.

A character's entire backstory is too much to cram into a movie, as is every detail about the fantasy universe the story takes place within. We cannot afford the page space to log their every thought, so we show the most important surface snippets and let the audience fill in the blanks. PASTO is no different. It just means we build more *behind our scenes* than may appear at first glance, and that focuses us on the dynamic that the audience becomes invested in. It may look like more work, but it actually makes writing scenes easier as it encourages us to focus on the mechanics and reasoning at play rather than trying to fill a vacuum with ad-libbed content. PASTO helps you get from point A to point B in the most entertaining way possible.

Example: In *Silence of the Lambs* (1991), Clarice Starling visits Dr Hannibal Lecter in his temporary holding cell in the Tennessee courthouse. She wants to work with Hannibal to identify the serial killer known as Buffalo Bill so she can save Catherine Martin, a missing woman Bill has recently kidnapped. Hannibal, however, has fallen for Clarice and wants to form an intimate relationship with her. Clarice enters the scene knowing she has already betrayed Hannibal with a fake prison transfer offer and tries to win him over by claiming she's visiting to return his precious drawings back to him.

Hannibal, himself, has read her case file and has prepared annotations to help her, but neither Clarice nor the viewer knows this. Hannibal opens by accusing Clarice of visiting to wheedle him into giving up information once again, quickly creating strong conflict between them. She counters by claiming she wants to be there for personal reasons, knowing full well that will appeal to him emotionally.

Hannibal engages in discussion about Buffalo Bill's motivations but, rather than give clear guidance, talks in riddles to drive down the clock and further frustrate Clarice. Eventually, Hannibal states she has nothing to barter for help other than sharing the most intimate secrets from her childhood. Clarice, in a moment of complete fragility, submits and reveals that she is haunted by the child-like screams of lambs she heard being slaughtered on the ranch she was sent to as an orphan.

Hannibal concludes this forms her entire motivation to save Catherine and, satisfied by knowing Clarice's deepest wound, hands over the case file she needs, stealing his first physical touch of her in the process of the exchange. Thus, he gives her the lead she desperately needs to pursue in her investigation, the catch being that they now have a relationship that is no longer just business.

Using PASTO and scene writing advice from a variety of sources I've collected over the years, I've developed everything into a single worksheet you'll find in this chapter. It's always worth filling one of these in before writing a first draft, even if you already have a good idea of what's going to happen. Not only will it trigger new ideas, but it will also serve as a holding place for notes.

Character and World Building Scenes

Some of our scenes will always lean toward exposition because they exist to establish our character and their world. Most of these types of scenes will be in the first act but may occur later on. What's important is that they have relevance, so the information they put across has some sort of payoff later on. Again, these scenes still need conflict and emotion and can still be well-structured with intentions, Turnarounds, and Outcomes. However, those intentions may not be strongly linked to the plot that's unfolding, especially when showing us the normal life of our protagonist before they've reached the tipping point that takes them into the second act.

Example: In the James Bond films (1954 onward), it's become a staple of each movie to show 007 meeting with the current Quartermaster (aka "Q") who heads up the highly advanced research and development department within the British Secret Intelligence Service. During this routine scene, which has existed in 21 of the 24 most recent Eon Productions James Bond films, Bond is shown various cutting edge spy devices and how they operate. This is all foreshadowing – as we know full well – 007 will be using them later; it's just a case of when and where. Despite this scene being almost pure exposition, there is often conflict there, typically the interpersonal kind between Bond's laissez-faire attitude to safety and cost, and Q being very uptight.

Action Scenes

Action should never really be just action. Much like opera, the sensation isn't the point; it's the highly entertaining mechanic being used to get the point across. Dialogue is great and can be incredibly high impact, but it requires mental energy to follow, and this can be draining when it isn't broken up by something more visceral.

Action, in the form of things such as hand-to-hand combat and car chases, activates the primal senses, which thrive on movement and sound. The stakes are high (injury or death) and the urgency immediate. However, action that fails to advance the story in a meaningful way can quickly become exhausting to watch; we soon start to ask ourselves, 'What's the point?' This is why some sub-genres, such as martial arts movies, car-sploitation cinema, and slasher films, tend to have a cult following – the fans are so into the action, a lack of story development won't bore them.

Writing well-structured action scenes is really no different to writing any other kind of well-structured scene; it's just that the dialogue and character moments are much more extreme. You can still use the PASTO system I propose where Preparation may be kicking a door down as a surprise, Action may be a sniper opening fire on their target, Struggle may be two fighters interlocked in a mutual hold, Turnaround may be a street racer hitting a hidden nitrous oxide switch, and Outcome may be a tortured hostage realising they have to save others while they desperately try to escape their captor.

Example: The all-time biggest example of drama within Action has to the famous moment in *Star Wars: Episode V – The Empire Strikes Back* (1980) when Luke Skywalker, trapped in the carbon-freezing chamber of Cloud City, runs into Darth Vader. They engage in a lightsaber duel atop a perilously narrow platform above an air chamber, and Vader manages to chop off Skywalker's hand and hold him at his mercy. As Skywalker backs away onto a tiny ledge, his importance and potential role in the Dark Side is alluded to by Vader, who eventually reveals he's his father. Accepting this horrible truth, Skywalker leaps from the ledge to what appears to be certain death.

Minor Distractions

One of the best reasons to use scene structure and establish our beats is to avoid the mistake of becoming distracted and having characters engage in behaviour that has no impact on the story. This is very easy to do, without direction, when we become immersed.

A lot of normal life is just filling in the silence with aimless chit-chat, but movies are supposed to be larger than life. Think about when you overhear conversations in a coffee shop. People talking about their last meal or shopping trip doesn't capture your attention at all, but someone ranting about some recent family drama will have you on the edge of your seat to hear what happened next.

There are, of course, exceptions when it comes to distractions, and they may even provide a welcome break from a highly serious plot. Some types of films, such as the "hangout movie" sub-genre, trade on the back of watching characters interact outside the plot, and thus these distractions can be their main appeal. The most common form of distraction that doesn't tend to compromise entertainment is delving into brief comedic skits. What shows particularly good craft is where the writer is able to weave theme into what seems like a distraction, and everything is still driving the story forward.

> **Example:** In *HotRod* (2007), an off-beat surreal comedy about a calamitous amateur motorcycle stuntman, a serious scene where Rod Kimble and Kevin Powell apologise to one another and clear their differences segues into repeating the line "cool beans" over and over in different ways. It becomes a farcical musical remix, quickly lifting the mood back up from something emotionally heavy and awkward. While the read was reportedly ad-libbed on the day, and edited to the point of madness later, it goes to show just how far left-of-left a scene can go for a few moments, providing it's entertaining and fits with the overall tone of the movie.

Slugs Aren't Scenes

Try not to think of slug lines denoting scenes in a story sense.

> A slugline is a heading we give each scene that quickly establishes the location and time of day along with other core factors such as the location itself being in motion (car, plane, boat, etc.), or the scene being out of chronological order (flashback, premonition, future, etc.).

Sure, they typically specify a scene during a shooting schedule, but a script is a very technical document. Sometimes a single contained scene isn't enough to contain the beats we need to fulfil our complete structure. In this case, we expand the structure outward – across multiple slugs – to effectively build the equivalent of a book chapter through a sequence of scenes.

If I look at my own scripts, I can see that I tend to use an average of six sequences per act (a total of around thirty per script) which can contain anything from one to four scenes but which mostly lean toward two.

You may also have location changes within a scene and thus have multiple slugs. If you have two characters locked in a war of words while walking outside, and those characters wander into a building, you use a new interior slug line as the location changes while the scene itself continues. This can also sometimes work the other way around when multiple scenes take place within the same location.

> **Example:** In *Rango* (2011), our hapless chameleon hero moseys into town and enters a saloon where he draws suspicion from intimidating clientele who demand to know who he is and where he's from. Realising he can choose any identity he fancies, he takes on the moniker "Rango" and claims to be from the "Far West", where strangers like him are considerably more dangerous.
>
> When asked if he's the person who killed the Jenkins brothers, he assures them he is and – in fact – only used one bullet to do so, despite there being seven of them, leading to him having to ad-lib a fantastical story of how the feat was achieved.
>
> Having convinced the locals, who applaud his tall tale, Bad Bill – a supporting antagonist – enters while terrorising one of the townsfolk

and gets into a confrontation with Rango. Despite seeming to be continuous, the first scene where Rango has to convince the locals 'who he is' ends just before Bad Bill enters, leading to a new scene where he proceeds to unwittingly taunt the outlaw into a showdown.

The flip side to of all this is where the structure is compressed down to little more than a quick series of shots and thus makes a montage. Here we shrink the structure inward, and those key scene beats become tiny moments.

Example: In season four of *Family Guy* (1999 onward), during the episode *Don't Make Me Over*, the 80s trope of including a montage where people fix things up is parodied when Peter Griffin and his friends decide to renovate their favourite bar in rapid time. For all the comic satire, the montage is well-structured, with the Preparation being their offer to help, the Action being them getting to work, the Struggle being all the mistakes they make along the way, the Turnaround being the big reveal that they've actually made the place look far worse, and the Outcome being that someone else is now going to have a harder time cleaning up their mess.

The tried and tested method for laying out scenes is by using an index card system. These notecards can be filled in with a heading and description then laid out and moved around as best suited for the story. Some writing software such as Scrivener includes a digital interpretation of this, while platforms such as Prewrite have been created to modernise and improve the process.

Trimming the Fat

The worksheet for this chapter should spark a lot of new creative ideas for your scenes, and it will be easy to add too much and overwrite. I encourage you to keep scenes as tight as possible, as ten seconds in movie time can feel like an hour when watching. Most scenes should be a few pages, at most, for the pace of a typical mainstream movie which aligns well with daily production constraints.

Something that can be very enlightening is to watch your favourite recent TV series with the stopwatch app open on your phone. Hit "Lap" every time a scene ends, and you'll get a log of scene lengths. You should find that the scenes, while packed with drama, actually go by very fast, almost always under two minutes and often shorter than one. Given that a script page tends to represent a minute of screen time, it goes to show just how long two or three pages really feels to the viewer. Now, your chosen pace is up to you, but it's important to appreciate what's common.

You'll most likely want to go back after your initial draft and trim the scenes down in length. Here are some tips on where to check for issues:

Repeated beats – Unless you need to really emphasise something, you can keep your characters moving through the scene without repeating themselves or the point they are making.

Chit-chat, back and forth, and formalities – Film is infamous for characters not saying goodbye on the phone before hanging up, but there's really no need for trivial moments that slow things down. There's no need for characters to "ping-pong" conversations back and forth either, like an elderly couple trying to communicate between the floors of their home.

Redundant characters – If a character has only one or two things to say or do in a scene, it might be worth cutting them out entirely. Your producer may hate you for requiring another actor for another day when they don't really do much, and the actor may hate you for giving them so little to work with.

Repeated information – Try to foreshadow without giving away what's coming up, and try to reference what's happened previously without repeating it in detail. While a character may not be up to speed, your audience is… and don't want to sit through what they already know.

Unnecessary detail – It's easy in some genres (such as sci-fi) to show off your world-building by having your characters talk about details that prove how much you've thought about things; often, these details aren't entertaining or dramatic to the audience. A lot of this might be better summarised or left unsaid unless "science porn" is key to the script's appeal, such as in a film like *The Martian*.

In some cases, you may find a scene that can be cut completely because the information it provides does little to move the story forward. This is fine. There's plenty going on in the lives of your characters that will not be shown.

Example: *Grey's Anatomy* (2005 onward) is primetime TV that's bordering on a soap opera. While the scenes are well-structured and packed with drama, they rarely run over a minute in length. *Moon* (2009), however – a cult film harking back to the pace of older science fiction movies – tends to have scenes the run from one to two minutes in length with very short moments shown between them. The former lends itself perfectly to the attention span of today's mainstream audience who need to switch off and unwind after work, while the latter feels almost snail's pace in comparison but is equally compelling and even relaxing for those who want to take their time and concentrate on something meaningful. There is no right or wrong nor better or worse artistically!

Finding balance here is a combination of logistical needs and personal taste. Many indie productions are constrained by a ninety-minute screener allowance at film markets, thus limiting the script to around ninety pages. Some assignment contracts issued by production companies to writers have an agreed page count range within them stated in black and white. Plus, of course, short scripts have the most imposing time constraints out there, such as contests that set the maximum run time at a mere three minutes.

This all said, it's essential not to lose the charm inherent in a script that may come from all those little details – that may bulk it out – but do make it special. It's easy to go too cold in an effort to maximise white space and take a script right back to its bare bones. I've seen new writers adamant they must get a script down to a certain page count by any means in a bid to either prove something to themselves or impress their peers. It's important to remember that what feels right in your heart may not always be justified with any logic that's immediately obvious to your brain.

It's also important to remember that what we're dealing with is intrinsically organic. Scenes rarely get filmed exactly as the script is written due to limitations on the day, along with actors ad-libbing new moments and discovering more natural or more amusing ways to button-up the ending. Some wiggle room is needed, and that's before we even get into the editing process and what will need to be left on the cutting room floor. With that in mind, it's worth keeping the meat in the middle, so to speak, with all your important beats together and uninterrupted; removing a moment that doesn't work or which needs to be cut to shave a little time off can be very tricky to do in the edit bay, particularly when you have characters moving around and interacting.

Turn & Burn Scene
Development Worksheet

WHAT NEEDS TO HAPPEN TO PROGRESS THE STORY?

WHAT DO THE CHARACTERS WANT?

WHAT'S IN THEIR WAY?

HOW DO THE CHARACTERS PREPARE TO GET WHAT
THEY WANT?

HOW DO THE CHARACTERS COME INTO CONFLICT?

HOW DOES THE CONFLICT BECOME MORE
CHALLENGING?

WHAT IS THE REVERSAL/REVELATION?

HOW DO THE CHARACTERS ADAPT AND GET WHAT
THEY WANT?

WHAT PRICE IS PAID?

WHAT IS THE OUTCOME AND NEW GOAL?

WHAT CHARACTER EXPOSITION AND DIMENSIONS
ARE SHOWN?

WHAT QUESTIONS HAVE BEEN PLANTED?

CONFLICT ENVIRONMENTAL/INTERNAL:

HERO CONTRAST PERSONAL/ENVIRONMENTAL:

THEME:

HOW CAN THE AUDIENCE EMOTIONALLY RELATE?

NOTES:

My Mistakes with Scene Writing

Like many film fans, I went into screenwriting with a basic feeling for how scenes should play out because I'd subconsciously absorbed so much over the decades. I had the simple stuff there, with some intent behind characters entering the scene, a reveal or Turnaround, and then some sort of Outcome. I mean, it was clumsy, but it was there.

However, almost everything was plot with a sprinkling of emotion. It was characters talking about what they needed to do next and how they were going to tackle it, or worse, talking about what they were already doing or had done. Occasionally, I would hit a vacuum – a scene where the characters had little to do or discuss – and thus, they would chat about random nonsense that was entertaining but had nothing to do with the story.

Oddly enough, it was actually through the villains that I really started to notice this; they were typically pursuing my protagonist and thus had nothing to discuss other than what food they wanted from a diner they'd stopped at, or which radio station they wanted to listen to in the car. None of this really built character or brought out the theme of the story. It was just idle chit-chat.

What beats I had were often repeated, too, as characters confirmed things and repeated themselves over and over.

Something I didn't realise I was doing at the time was adding in additional characters (often quite wacky ones) into pretty much every scene, so the existing characters had someone to bounce off and do something interesting. They were always doing something like checking into a motel, placing an order with a server, or arguing with a gas station clerk. None of it was boring, but little of it fitted into a bigger picture that elevated the story.

My action scenes were epic, though. Like Indiana Jones-level scope with lots of neat twists and turns, but – again – *no real substance* behind the beats. Just people winning and losing. Being a petrolhead, I could write vehicle chases all day long and did just that, motivated by doing the stunts justice rather than doing the story justice. I wrote one early script that had next-to-no character development (and certainly no theme) but consisted of one huge action sequence after the next. I thought it would compensate. It didn't.

I was reading a lot of books, but still, the only craft advice out there was to *enter late and leave early,* which I appreciated, but it didn't really help me much because I was already keeping things pretty tight. Something that had impacted me early on was Craig Mazin and John August discussing scene length on their *Scriptnotes* podcast and mentioning that anything over a couple of pages was a long scene, partly because there's only so much you can shoot in one day. I know that for myself, having watched my own scenes being shot and seeing just how many takes are needed to get all the coverage. Needless to say, now that I'm producing too, I'm more than aware that time is money.

The big revelation came via a working writer giving advice on a forum. They suggested using the PASTO system, which I was highly sceptical of at first. I'm always resistant to academic thinking, so it's actually pretty hilarious that I'm now writing a book on craft.

PASTO really got me thinking about what mattered, especially when combined with the many different types of conflict I was becoming aware of, along with the need to always leverage as much emotion as possible. I ended up putting the knowledge I'd gathered, and reflected upon, all together into the worksheet included in this chapter and forced myself to slow down a little and complete one for *every* scene before I started drafting.

The difference it made to the dramatic impact of my scene writing was remarkable, and improvements were instantaneous. I was overwhelmed by ideas and improvements. My scenes had more intention behind them, with every character battling it out through their relationships and emotional needs. In fact, I've had other writers comment to me since that "I never let my characters off the hook", and that's true. It's something I'm proud of. They don't get a break, and they work their hardest from the first page to the last, which they damn well should do to entertain the audience and earn their ending.

Of course, combining this with the boot camp I put myself through – writing short scripts for a few years – particularly emphasised the need to make every beat count, since every line is so precious when your entire story is only half a dozen pages long.

This new approach to scene writing also caused me to revisit features with a whole new desire. I started writing dialogue-heavy single-location thrillers. No car chases. No stunt spectaculars. Just characters mostly talking for ninety minutes and making that as engaging as possible. Some of my proudest and most highly-acclaimed scripts are these micro-budget features which directors have told me they'd cut vital parts of their anatomy off to shoot scenes from, and readers have told me 'do so much with so little' that they could be played out on stage.

I also went back and ran some of my older material through the system and – Wow! – I soon found out where the deadwood was, and what some scenes needed to make them pop. My characters talked a lot less about what they needed to do too. They talked a lot less about what was going on around them and about technical information, as well. Instead, they started talking about what mattered to them, with a strategy to achieve something meaningful.

My action scenes improved radically, too, because they now had the drama behind the dramatic. A shootout wasn't just a shootout anymore; it was a huge step forward for my hero in terms of discovering who they are and what really matters in life. It was a vital part of their journey, not just logistically but spiritually. Now they were taking a literal leap of faith.

What I love most, though, about my deep understanding of scene structure is that I can sit with an actor on set and explain *why* their character is doing what they are doing. They say acting is reacting, and sure, that's true. But acting is fundamentally behaving with intent, and that intent needs to be motivated by a desire. It also means that I can handle any emergency rewrites on set (such as line changes or cutting down pages) to speed up shooting without worrying that I'm breaking the scene in some way. Plus, I can carry that same awareness through to the editing suite, if I'm involved in that capacity.

Please understand that I genuinely use this worksheet for my own writing even now, years later, in a professional capacity. I find it incredibly powerful, even as the guy who created it. I am constantly pleased with the results and, although it means more work upfront, it means far less time spent trying to break down and fix what doesn't work later on.

Something I've come to learn during my adventures in writing is that great art, as chaotic and organic as the result often appears, has structure behind its creation. I've yet to see a highly successful artist who doesn't have some sort of process or "method behind the madness", which they utilise each time. A good process doesn't reduce creativity as I feared would; it simply channels all that creative energy into the areas it's needed the most.

Now, with that said, we have all our beats. So, let's talk about putting some words in our characters' mouths.

CHAPTER 5: DIALOGUE

When the topic of writing better dialogue comes up, the response is often focused on the surface level of speech (how it sounds) rather than the motivation behind the speech (what it means). Better dialogue is really a combination of the two, and you may have found you are already more competent in one area than the other. You do, however, need to master both.

More Realistic Dialogue

This is really the art of the mimic, and all down to your ability to pick up on how different people talk. Rhythm, patter, and flow are some factors, but so is the choice of wording people tend to use. Much like any set of mannerisms, they are complex and often nuanced. If you are good at connecting with many different kinds of people through conversation, you have probably found you have a chameleon-like ability to adapt your speech so you can relate.

This all comes down to being a good listener, a sponge that retains the essence of personality as you experience it, which is an essential part of being a relatable storyteller. Unless you've been living under a rock with zero exposure to pop culture for your entire life, you already have this ability in some capacity, believe me.

Thankfully, you can exploit this imitation part of your brain to write more realistic-sounding dialogue, which helps give your characters their own unique sounding voice. The hack is to simply have the people you can imitate well 'play' your characters in your head as you write. You don't have to be able to perfectly imitate them vocally, just be able to imitate them on the page. Those people can be anyone you choose… from family and friends to actors and reality TV stars. All that matters is that you're familiar with how they talk.

Let's have a little play with this for a beat that seems pretty innocuous. Suddenly, "I'd like a caramel latte and a ham and cheese panini, please" when ordering in a coffee shop becomes…

Character #1 (inspired by Samuel L Jackson) "Hey, how you doin'? A caramel latte, if you may, and how about one of those ham and cheese paninis?"

Character #2 (inspired by Sandra Bullock) "Morning! Can I get a caramel latte? Please… and maybe a ham and cheese panini too? Thank you!"

Character #3 (inspired by Jack Nicholson) "Caramel latte, ham and cheese panini. Thanks, I appreciate it."

Character #4 (inspired by Kristen Stewart) "Hey umm, can I get like, a caramel latte? Oh, and a ham and cheese panini! Thanks so much!"

Okay, it's unlikely I'm not going to be ghostwriting for any of the Hollywood elite any time soon, but I'm sure you catch my drift – same intent, four very different ways of delivering it. This is how you give characters a unique voice so they sound different to one another and don't always sound like you. I strongly recommend you take a good look at who you often find yourself naturally imitating, which is a lot easier if you've already written a few scripts. You may find you have some go-to people that crop up quite often. Lean into that.

More Dramatic Dialogue

This side of dialogue is less talked about, but it's where the rubber really meets the road. Dramatic dialogue is where *intent* collides with *challenge*, and thus we get conflict. The dynamic behind the interaction makes it compelling to witness in real-time as our brains engage on an intellectual and emotional level.

Think about the dullest conversations you've had in your life, the most painstaking and drawn out, if you can remember them. They were most likely during situations where neither you – nor those you were trying to converse with – had any good reason to talk, other than to fill a void of silence. Introverts will especially know the pain of making small talk with strangers. Other painful conversations will probably include those which were one-sided, where someone dumped a stream of information on you in which you held little value in knowing, or put any information into extracting. On the flip-side, the conversations which really stick in your mind are most likely arguments, debates, and discussions that you were passionately invested in at the time. Asking a crush if they would like to go on a date, a boss if they can give you a raise, or a parent to accept your sexuality aren't necessarily pleasurable conversations to approach, or navigate, but they come with high stakes and adversity that make them truly memorable by default. Just think about the conversations from your past that still circle in your head when you try to sleep at night. Why has your brain chosen to preserve and dwell on those moments? It's because what was said *mattered*.

This is the real problem I most often see behind a screenwriter's dialogue issues. It's not that the speech itself is clunky, it's just that the characters have no good reason to talk other than to state the obvious. The result tends to be scenes where everybody is simply trying to get from A to B with characters attempting to fill the void with small talk about what's going on around them (usually the plot), or worse still, relaying exactly what the audience just watched unfold in the scene prior before discussing what they're about to do in the scene that's coming up. There is no immediacy nor suspense. I call this type of dialogue 'toddler talk' because it reads like someone playing a make-believe game with a child – "Oh no! We need to cross the bridge! I hope we don't fall!"; "Wow! We made it! Quick! Cut the rope so they can't follow us!"; "Oh no! Look! They're in a helicopter! Let's run to that cave!" Generally, I've found infants have little time for philosophical musings within the narrative of their fictional adventures.

This is why knowing all the beats for our scenes is so important because it gives us the motivation behind the character's need to say anything. Dialogue – even that which is said with zero passion or personality – is simply a lot more interesting when there's drama behind the words.

Example: In *The Matrix* (1999-2003), the computer system that's created the virtual world Neo is living in can enter at any time in the form of Agent Smith, a man in sunglasses and a business suit. Smith, a personification of artificial intelligence, talks in a highly monotone way devoid of any emotion and tends to monologue, as the feelings and opinions of others are inconsequential to him. Despite this, Agent Smith has us hanging off every word because of the significance of what he has to say in terms of both plot and theme. Smith is the main antagonist, after all, but his determination to destroy Neo also comes with some damning opinions on the human race.

Let's go back to our characters and add conflict to their situation…

Character #1 (finding nobody at the counter) "Hey, hello? Anyone in today? Service please?"

Character #2 (distracted by point of sale) "Oh man, do you have to put the paninis on display like that? I'm trying to stick to a diet here!"

Character #3 (alienated by product line) "What exactly is a caramel latte, anyway? What's wrong with regular coffee? Why's everything gotta be a dessert now?"

Character #4 (discovering a stock issue) "Dude, I need sugar and caffeine, like, so much right now. You cannot be out of syrup."

Now we have dialogue that's in a unique voice and going somewhere because behind it is that *beat*, a moment that carries our story forward because it has purpose.

However, we can go deeper than that by incorporating theme as well, by bringing each character's perspective onto the subject at hand. This isn't necessarily something that's done in an obvious way. It can be anything from subtext to off-handed comments to full-blown monologues.

Theme stems from our character's own belief system, so we need to have an idea of *what that is* before we can have them communicate it.

Let's go back to the coffee shop and have our characters continue to talk while throwing in some life-affirming values, such as our individual relationship with destiny…

> Character #1 (believing life puts up obstacles) "Seriously? Well, ain't that the truth! Just when a man needs sustenance the most, suddenly everyone's on some union downtime bullshit!"
>
> Character #2 (believing life spites them) "You know, it's weird. Too weird. I start a new diet and you guys have precisely what I can't eat on offer the next day. Which one of you bugged my house? Is it you? It's you, isn't it? I recognise you."
>
> Character #3 (believing life is out to destroy them) "So, now I gotta worry about my heart rate AND my cholesterol when all I wanted is a pick me up. Is it me or is corporate America trying to kill us all off? Who benefits from that? Am I the only one here NOT getting my card stamped for this suicide pact?"
>
> Character #4 (believing life is fatalistic) "Fine, whatever, I knew it. I knew the second I decided I was gonna treat myself, it wasn't gonna work out. I don't care. I'm over it already. That's just like, my tragic little life."

Now, we're really saying something, all over something seemingly trivial!

To summarise, better dialogue requires us to hone a wide set of skills and combine our ability to build characters, story theme, and scene structure with our knack of taking someone's voice and channelling our own through it. Ultimately, it is us that's speaking, but we're doing in the most entertaining way we can by having a variety of interesting characters speak for us as they battle through their own existences. This way, not only does our dialogue feel richer, it feels like it is based in a much bigger universe where even something as mundane as ordering lunch can deliver just enough conflict to reveal someone's entire view on life itself.

Finding Those Missing Voices

Sometimes, there isn't a person for us to find inspiration from in our heads. The good news is you don't have to go out into the big wide world or cycle through endless TV shows in the hope of running into the right person to 'voice' a character. You can easily go through YouTube to find people that fit. This can be particularly useful for more technical dialogue such as law enforcement, pilot chatter, or legal discourse. It's also good for dialect – particularly old-fashioned dialect – that you're unlikely to ever hear around you day-to-day.

Trust the Voice in Your Head

Something I've come to learn from watching actors perform my writing is to trust the voice in your head over the one in your throat.

A lot of writers state that we have to be able to perform our dialogue out loud to prove it works. The fact is, most of us are not performers, and therefore – because of our individual speech patterns – we may not be best suited to delivering our lines. Yes, I appreciate how crazy that sounds on the surface. Go and read some Shakespeare and see how natural, clear, and dramatic you can make it, even after numerous attempts. Now go and listen to a professional rendition of the same lines on YouTube. Unless you're a budding thespian, you probably made the same sentences sound like a muffled tongue twister while the professionals made them sound like poetry.

This is a huge part of what highly skilled actors do; they deliver lines with exceptional rhythm and clarity. What's more important is that your characters maintain their distinct voices throughout the script and that they don't all sound the same. Sure, by all means, say your lines out loud to yourself when writing – if it helps – but also have faith in your ability to write for others and trust the process when it comes to shooting. Also, accept that actors will sometimes deliver something better than you ever imagined because your voice, plus the character's voice, plus the actor's voice equals something really remarkable. Some writers simply gel with some actors.

As you get better at having real people play your characters in your head, you'll hopefully reach a position where you are able to write for specific actors because you've studied their speech patterns enough to know what they need. This can become a very powerful skill if you're ever closely involved in the pre-production of a script and know who will be cast in certain roles. You can then make tweaks to suit those performers. If you haven't been exposed to a lot of their work, I suggest going through the actor's reel over and over. This will show the performances they are most proud of, and you can study their voice until you're able to recreate it in your head and make tweaks to your production draft.

Spell It Out for Them

The cast are going to do their best to interpret your words, and you can make it a lot easier for them by spelling everything out – even something as simple as number sequences – so the rhythm and or use feels correct, e.g., "Turn 180°" can be interpreted as "Turn one-eighty" or "Turn a hundred and eighty degrees" or "Turn one-eight-zero" depending on the style and tone someone chooses when reading it. Don't leave it up for debate, especially if it's technical jargon that may make the actor and entire production look foolish, should they get it wrong.

When developing one of my scripts with a director, there was a little debate over the common pronunciation of "Roth IRA". The director felt it was normal to say "Roth eye-rah" while I was more familiar with "Roth eye-arr-aye". After some research into today's common use, we decided to go with the latter and had it written as "Roth I.R.A." in the script to make it clear how we preferred the actor to pronounce it.

Following on from the above, it's worth noting people rarely extrapolate an initialisation and say "Roth individual retirement account", but people typically do when reading "mph", which they'll extrapolate into "miles per hour". Again, when in doubt, spell it out!

Parentheticals

The role of a parenthetical (the text in brackets above lines of dialogue in a script sometimes known as *wrylys*) is to give context to lines. For example, it's pretty much impossible to communicate sarcasm in words alone, and thus that tone of speech always benefits from a parenthetical. Tone isn't the only context that may be needed, however. A character may make an observation, address a specific person, or redirect a conversation, and thus this needs a reference via parentheticals such as (re: the accounting issue), (to Amanda), (back to subject). Another common use for parentheticals is where a character is talking into a device such as a phone, bullhorn, or radio. E.g., (into phone), (into bullhorn), (into radio).

Poor use of parentheticals is typically associated with writers trying to specify the nature of how lines are delivered, and this is often an over-step into the director's and actor's territory. Not only will they have their own take on how the lines should be spoken, they will be in character during a performance and reacting as naturally as possible.

Generally speaking, it's best to use as few parentheticals as possible, as they are a technical tool rather than a creative one.

> **Example:** The pilot script for *Lost* (2004-2010) contains pretty much every use of a parenthetical imaginable within the first ten pages and does so in a way that adds urgency, emotion, and humour to the script. Uses during the opening chaos, where we follow Dr Jack Shephard trying to deal with the aftermath of a plane crash on the shore of a tropical island, include (searching for his wife), (looks up, calls out:), (with bedside manner, to Claire), and (just get the fuck outta here).

Subtext

You know when people say, "Show, don't tell"? Well, subtext is a bigger part of that than it's given credit for. As human beings, we rarely feel comfortable saying exactly what we want to say (aka being 'On the nose'), and the true message we are conveying is often buried between the lines. This can make listening to people's conversations fascinating as we use tone and context to establish what's really being said. It's absolutely possible to write a dialogue-heavy script that never really tells the audience anything outright and instead expects them to decipher the true meaning.

> **Example:** In *Twilight* (2008), the first thing we hear Bella Swan's father say to her during an awkward car ride is, "Your hair's longer." to which she replies, "I cut it since last time I saw you." His comment suggests he's trying hard to connect with her, while her reply tells us that he's not been paying enough attention to her, and she's prepared to call him out indirectly.

For me, the key to writing subtext comes back to having a healthy scene dynamic in place. Our characters need to be navigating scenes with a chess-like strategy. Once we know every beat of the scene, every little play and reaction, then we know what the characters are trying to do. By knowing what they are trying to do, we can then add a layer of normality that seems more like everyday life over the top of that dynamic. Working this way around makes writing realistic dialogue and action a lot easier.

> **Example:** In *Margin Call* (2011), Sarah Robertson, a board member who's been chosen by the jeopardised investment firm to be fired as a symbolic sacrifice, sits with Eric Dale, a recently fired risk analyst who predicted the financial meltdown they are facing, as they wait for the markets to open and their traders to desperately sell off all the company's holdings.
>
> Faced with unemployment after years of loyalty to the firm, Robertson asks Dale a simple question, "Do you have kids?" to which he replies, "Yes." Nothing else is said, and only Robertson's indifferent reaction is lingered upon, the subtext being that she has forgone having children for the sake of her career and is now calculating if the sacrifice was worth it.
>
> *Margin Call*, Oscar-nominated for its writing, is a masterclass in subtext with some of its most important moments either left unsaid or summed up in a few words, such as the Head of Trading, Sam Rogers, responding to CEO John Tuld's lengthy final speech about their current crisis being no different than any other in history with little more than the words, "I need the money" as the only reason he'll stay with the firm another two years. The statement not only serves as an important beat in his storyline (Rogers wants to do the right thing and leave, but he's trapped) but also a thematic summary of every character's flawed outlook on life (they are all acting the way they are, good or otherwise, because of their servitude to money).

This all said, learning to turn direct statements into normal conversations laced with context takes some practice. The worksheet included in this chapter is a system I developed very early on to help me turn 'on the nose' dialogue into something more subtle.

Dunna Be Worryin', Pet, Dialect's Optional, Innit?

While there's a lot of strong opinions for (and against) writing in a dialect, your decision to do so is entirely a stylistic one and up to you. Done well, dialogue written exactly as it's intended to be pronounced can add a lot of charm and colour to a script. Done badly, it will be a struggle to read through and understand.

On the flip side, dialogue written without any kind of edge or flair can come across as robotic and weak. As with many things in life, a balance is best found that preserves readability, feels vibrant, and gives actors enough direction to deliver what's needed. Go with what works best for you.

> **Example:** *Peaky Blinders* (2012 onward), set in Birmingham, England, is famed for its strong use of the distinct post-world-war-one 'Brummy' accent, which can be tough for people to understand. The scripts for the show, however, give little indication of this and, without context, could easily be interpreted to be in whatever accent the reader defaults to. *No Country For Old Men* (2007) goes completely the other way; the heavy deep-south drawl of its characters right there – and unmistakable on the page – has lines such as "I'm fixin' to do somethin' dumbern hell but I'm goin' anyways." Neither is better or worse for it.

Too Much Dialogue

At some point in your early writing life, particularly if you solicit feedback from other amateurs, someone is going to tell you that your characters talk too much. I've even seen writers go as far as telling others that this is the case based on a high page count alone. The truth is, if someone doesn't like your style or becomes disengaged with your script, they are going to grow tired of your characters talking. Remember, there are plenty of people who find the work of multiple academy award winner Aaron Sorkin "too wordy".

The dialogue you do need to worry about is superfluous dialogue; characters talking about things that are obvious, unrelated to the story, or overly detailed. There's nothing wrong with dialogue-heavy scriptwriting, providing that dialogue has purpose and is written in an engaging way.

> **Example:** The opening scene of *Inglourious Basterds* (2009) is set in Nazi-occupied France, where Col. Hans Landa of the SS visits farmer Perrier LaPadite – who he suspects is hiding Jews from his capture. It is around fifteen pages of pure talking between just two characters, and sections of dialogue often run ten lines deep and sometimes as many as thirty. It is, however, exceptionally captivating as every line reveals something more about the seemingly charming

but villainous colonel we are dealing with, the terrifying situation that's slowly unravelling for the farmer, and the Jewish family hiding under his floorboards.

Turn & Burn Scene
Subtext Worksheet

WHAT IS THE MOST LITERAL VERSION OF WHAT THE CHARACTER IS SAYING?

WHAT IS THE EXACT OPPOSITE VERSION OF WHAT THE CHARACTER IS SAYING?

WHAT IS THE MOST ABSURD VERSION OF WHAT THE CHARACTER IS SAYING?

THE ABOVE COMBINED INTO SOMETHING MORE REALISTIC:

My Mistakes with Dialogue

If there's one talent I walked into screenwriting with, it was being able to write realistic dialogue. I was a natural at it. My early screenplays flowed well with vibrant, unique voices to the characters who often had great one-liners and powerful monologues. I was so good at dialogue, in fact, that professional coverage readers would say that some of my writing had a certain poeticism to them and read like early Tarantino scripts. Needless to say, this was a huge compliment to receive at the time, and I (foolishly) rode on that for years.

However, my confidence when it came to realistic dialogue distracted me from an underlying issue; I wasn't as good as I could be when it came to dramatic dialogue. My blindspot was the fact that my dialogue was dramatic in terms of the wording and emotion, and this was distracting me from the lack of structure behind those words. The beats were missing or underdeveloped, and I couldn't see that because I didn't appreciate good scene structure, character development, and theme. The result was me being left in a state of complete confusion – I knew my characters spoke well, but I also knew what they were saying wasn't profound.

I kept thinking more poetic dialogue would compensate and couldn't work out why that wasn't working until I studied the craft of storytelling and realised how important it is to develop those beats; dialogue, no matter how crude, will always have impact when it adds drama in the form of progressing the plot, building the character, and communicating theme.

So, I stopped obsessing about HOW my characters were talking and started obsessing about WHY my characters were talking. This was like finding out that an engine needs a perfect 'stoichiometric' mix of fuel and air to maximise performance. I was no longer running too rich and choking myself; I was leaning things out a little and adding some vital oxygen that gave a bigger bang. The result? More power under my right foot, or perhaps more accurately, under each of my fingertips.

I'm pleased to say that I now get compliments on my dialogue from long-time directors and highly respected actors. In fact, there's at least one director-producer out there in Ho-Ho-Wood, as he calls it, who likes to tell people that nobody in the business can write female villains like CJ Walley. Quite the compliment to live up to.

The obstacles I do continue to run into revolve almost entirely around all the subtle differences between British English and American English. Despite the fact I now talk and spell in an eccentric fusion of the two languages, I still get caught out by slight differences now and then.

During the production of my first feature film, actors would keep approaching the director out of my earshot, in a state of confusion, wanting to know what on Earth the word "erm" could possibly mean when it was dotted within the dialogue. "He means 'umm'" the director would automatically respond. "The Brit says it differently, apparently." And it's true. We do say it differently.

In fact, being on set is possibly the greatest boot camp a writer can get when it comes to dialogue. There's no getting away from having to sit there, perched on an apple box beside the monitors, cringing in perpetual fear as you have to watch people attempt to speak your words right in front of you. No escape.

Something that hits you right away is just how incredibly good actors are at turning even the dullest sentences into compelling speech. Yes, it's their job to do so, but they are genuinely amazing at it, and you soon see how much better they are than yourself at mastering the rhythm and enunciation when you rehearse with them prior to a scene.

Another great benefit of being on set is being able to spot when you're giving them a sentence that feels like chewing gum to them. It happens. Sometimes the patter isn't quite right for that particular actor, and well, sometimes you just miss the mark slightly during the writing. It's a wonderful feeling to be able to jump in during a read or between takes and tell the actor just what slight modification is needed to make their life infinitely easier. And yeah, some actors, the more established ones, will make their own adjustments. Some will even go as far as to always rewrite every line they have, because they are excellent writers themselves and know what will work best for them. That's when it's great to be able to clearly see and communicate the beats of the scene, and how they work, should there be any concern that important moments might be missed. In situations like this, you have to put your ego aside and trust them. Filmmaking is a collaborative effort, and writers too precious about their words can easily become a hindrance to the production and the morale of the cast. Actors live for those moments of discovery, so let them have them! Even better, tell them upfront that you encourage it. It will be a beautiful day's shooting for them, I guarantee it.

Some actors build on lines too. By far my most on-the-spot moment when it comes to writing dialogue was during the filming of my first feature film assignment *Break Even*. We had secured Steve Guttenberg in the role of Lance and, being a child of the 80s, I got to meet one of my heroes and huge stars from that era.

Steve was a really friendly guy to meet and had a tremendous energy about him during his takes, changing things up as much as possible, and adding little moments to his character. We came to shoot his final scene where he talks about the movie's villain, DEA Agent Crowe, a woman his character had a romantic interest in, and knew better than anyone else. Steve took in the set around him – the workshop used for a few seasons of *Pimp My Ride* filled with classics and supercars – and felt there was a metaphor there for him to make in regard to Crowe and the restored Mercedes parked next to a brand new GT40 – he just needed the line.

All eyes then turned to me.

With my heart racing as fast as my mind, I managed to come up with something right there and then. "You know, most people think she's like that, a classic, but she really is a machine like that, she spits flames." Steve pointed right at me and exclaimed, "Yes! YES!" with delight. Talk about a rush. That's extreme sports for screenwriters! It's also the job and the kind of situation we need to be prepared for.

Something I've come to terms with (that used to bother me a little) was my frequent use of monologues. I love monologues, and love writing them, but I do appreciate that they are indulgent. Many amateur writers poo-poo them, and I've certainly read through some stinkers myself (I once read an amateur spec script with a seven-page monologue!). My concern was more to do with actors being able to remember them and the impact that may have on production if they kept fluffing takes.

A good monologue performed well can really be a glorious moment. In fact, during the casting of one of our movies, my director and producing partner, Shane Stanley, went to see a potential attachment for the villain. Right there, in the restaurant, she performed her monologue about Hooters waiting staff and mutual exploitation... from memory. I'm guessing she liked it.

I continue to always keep an ear out for great dialogue in the way strangers speak to one another around me. Sometimes it does a full loop and comes back to me. Once, I was standing in a queue at a local bakery and couldn't help but overhear a conversation taking place in front of me between a mother and her children. They were getting a little bored of waiting, and she was doing a great job of explaining why they needed to be patient not just for her sake but for everyone around them. She used the phrase "You've got my head crackling like bacon" to describe how stressed she was feeling, and I loved that expression. Later that day, someone on social media reached out and asked if it was me queuing behind them in the bakery earlier, as they thought they recognised me. "Head crackling like bacon?" I replied to their surprised delight.

And, hey, look, when you don't get the lines perfect the first time, it's easy to beat yourself up and feel like you've failed, especially when it happens on set as an actor you admire twists their mouth awkwardly around the words and loses focus. But dig this. Go and read the scripts for your favourite movies – while watching them – and notice how many little tweaks were made during production. The one that always stands out to me the most is the final line in the opening scene of *Pulp Fiction*, where Pumpkin and Honey Bunny decide to start robbing restaurants instead of their usual targets. The screeching of Honey Bunny as she whips out her revolver on the unsuspecting diners is probably burned into the minds of every film fan in the world who know it as, "Any of you fucking pricks move, and I'll execute every last mother-fucking one of you!" whereas, in the script, it's written as "Any of you fucking pricks move and I'll execute every one of you mother-fuckers! Got that?"

Now, we know two different versions were used as a quirky little easter egg when the ending of the scene is replayed later in the movie, but it's those last two words – "Got that?" – which were cut and created a line so iconic it was used in pop music.

There are two lessons to take there; firstly, even the best of the best when it comes to dialogue (like Tarantino himself) doesn't get it perfect on the page, and secondly, you should always be willing to make those little tweaks to elevate a performance.

To conclude my own lessons on dialogue, I'd say that learning to write dialogue is more about listening than speaking, and the most important parts of 'what needs to be said' often fall between the lines.

If you are working through this guide in sequence and developing a project as you go, you should now have pretty much everything you need to write a script – from your major plot points to character arcs to beats within scenes and the words which move the story forward. However, before you commit to drafting, I want to encourage you to look at what I call *pre-writing* because it revolutionised my process.

CHAPTER 6: DRAFTING

I'm going to make what may sound like a ridiculous statement; the worst way to write a story is to take a blank sheet of paper and start typing in paragraphs from the top left. Yeah, I know – odd take.

Please hear me out.

I cannot think of a single form of the creative arts where the creator launches out of the gate trying to nail the fine detail and maintain a high level of perfectionism all the way along a course they've yet to set, and a finish line they cannot see. It's madness, yet this is how most new writers go into drafting and, just to make it all a little crazier, go in with the intention to re-tread that journey over and over – sometimes just as blind each time – until they have something worthwhile.

Imagine trying to perfectly paint a blank canvas by starting in the top corner and having little to no idea what the final image will be. No thought about proportions. No consideration of colour palette. No establishment of movement. Imagine trying to write a piece of music note by note, covering every element and instrument in each bar with little regard for the overall phrasing or soundscape. It sounds ridiculous, and so it should.

Established artists of all kinds "sketch" or "rough out" in some form by getting their overall vision correct first and building in detail across the board, bit-by-bit, creating a deeper resolution each pass while maintaining an overview. They don't move forward unless the bigger picture looks/sounds/feels right, and thanks to this sketching mentality, they're able to make fundamental changes very easily in those early stages without having to undo a lot of effort.

When we draft, we are trying to un-muddle a creative mind that's obsessed with little more than an abstract. We kind of know the story, and we can kind of see and hear the story, but we cannot make out any firm detail when we try to look closer. In many cases, what we have is something that behaves like an M.C. Escher painting in our heads; the deeper we stare into certain parts, the less it makes sense overall. Like a concept designer dreaming up a new car, we need to figure out how many wheels and doors this thing needs before we obsess over the layout of the headlights and the colour of the seat stitching, else we are in danger of creating something akin to "The Homer" from the *Oh Brother, Where Art Thou?* episode of *The Simpsons*.

I think what causes us to adopt this arduous process is the perception of how successful writers draft. We hold onto an idealistic image of our writing heroes strumming the keys of an old typewriter as a butcher's roll of gleaming white paper flows steadily into the rollers, like something on a production line, emerging coated with perfect poetic prose. And it's fair to say that some highly revered authors do, in fact, write like that. But it's also important to remember just how long they've been writing for. Steven King started writing fiction at seven-years-old and has written nearly every day of his life since. With over two hundred penned stories to his name in the form of novels, short stories, and novellas, it's fair to say he's going in with a mind that's trained to do a lot of that "sketching" instinctively.

You have probably heard the Picasso's Napkin story before, but now's the time to think about what it really says about artistic development. In the story, Picasso is relaxing in a Parisian cafe when a fan spots him and – knowing that prior to being famous he would often draw quick sketches on napkins for waitresses in the hope of a free dinner in return – she asks him if he can draw and sign something on a napkin for her. Picasso, more than happy to oblige, grabs a napkin, doodles something right there and then, adds his signature, and asks her for a small fortune in exchange for it. Flummoxed by his request for payment, she exclaims, "How can you ask for so much? It only took you a minute to draw this!" and he retorts, "No, it took me 40 years." The message to take away from this story is that those who've honed their talent over decades, to the point it's instinctive, will make the process look easy. By example, think about a trapeze artist being able to effortlessly somersault from one performer's grip into another's (after spending years familiarising themselves with the basics while wearing safety harnesses and swinging mere feet above the ground). When a new writer attempts to write a perfect draft on a clean sheet of paper, it's no different to them standing on a tall platform, grabbing the ropes, and hoping for the best as they swing above the crowd with only a vague idea of the stunts they desire to pull off, and if there's anyone else out there to catch them.

If there is one axiom I cannot abide by in the screenwriting world, it's the phrase "rewriting is writing". It is often uttered in a therapeutic, high-pitched, cult-like tone by writers lost in the development soup of their own spec script. Writers who are now suffering the writing equivalent of Stockholm Syndrome as they dive back in for yet another shot at the brass ring. So, I would like you to consider an alternative phrase... *pre-writing is writing*!

Introducing the Scriptment

We have to drop the idea that we are creative printers that churn out material from a spool. The typewriter is dead and we are writers, not typists. The fundamental problem we are creating for ourselves is a nasty combination of pressure, doubt, and fear. We are trying to write the perfect sentence while unsure if the moment is even needed, and with no firm idea of what's coming next. We are ad-libbing while hoping for a perfect rendition with the caveat that we can have unlimited do-overs. We have no scope of the overall task at hand, and every step only serves to make things more complicated and permanent. It's impossible to focus on every brick you lay full-on when you're unsure of the layout of the building and worried you might later have to knock down the entire wall.

There is a better and much more simple way to approach drafting, and that's to work in lists of bullet points. If you're using a story structure, then simply bullet point the key sections (e.g., Yearn, Learn, Turn, Burn, Earn) and add more bullet points under those sections (e.g., Tipping Point, Point of No Return, Point of Realisation, Point of Acceptance) until your page turns into pages. Let acts become sequences, let sequences become scenes, and let scenes become beats as you establish one level and go down the next.

Have a great line or moment in your head as you go along? Boom! Add it as a bullet point and move on. Don't spend time refining it. Focus on the bigger picture until you know you're definitely going to need it. Gone down the wrong path with an idea? No problem! Bullet points are easy to go in and adjust, so less to worry about in terms of committing material to the page. Feeling motivated to work on that action sequence at the bottom of the fourth act? Fill your boots! Go in and add a series of bullet points detailing how the action plays out. You don't have to work in order anymore.

Once you have all your basics in place, you can start adding slug lines where your scenes begin and replace an idea for a line with a properly formatted piece of character dialogue. What you're creating here is what's known as a *Scriptment*.

You are, I hope, familiar with what a script looks like and, if you've read through the previous chapters, should have an idea of how a treatment is like a long synopsis for a script idea. Well, a scriptment is a hybrid of the two, which is less refined than a script but more detailed than a treatment. It's an organic document that can be written using screenwriting software as it gradually morphs from a set of basic notes into a completed and fully-formatted script.

What you are effectively creating with a bullet-pointed scriptment is a to-do list for your first proper draft. This works exceptionally well with something like the Turn & Burn system because you can take all those beats you've created using the worksheets and simply copy and paste them into your document for each scene. By having all this in place first, you can eventually go in and focus on the fine detail and flowery prose, knowing you have the fundamentals in place.

This should all result in an incredibly strong first draft that doesn't need to be broken down, analysed, or rewritten over and over, because you've taken the time to get the foundations and framework in order before committing to the detail. Overall, the process should not only be more efficient, but it should also be more enjoyable because you're giving yourself permission to indulge in what matters *when it matters* rather than creating in a constant paradoxical state of rigorously engineered structure and hedonistic dreamy visualisation. Don't lock yourself in purgatory. Write smarter, not harder. There's no Oscar for writing the most drafts or hitting the highest word count. The most creative artists win.

Something I also strongly recommend throughout this process, and which works really well to help stay motivated, is to make a run through the script to get your basic bullet points in place and change the text colour before you go through making adjustments and adding another layer of detail. This really helps show you how much progress you are making and how this all adds up. Keep doing this as your scriptment grows into a fully-formatted script, and you should end up with something that looks like a festival of Christmas lights, each colour representing the sketch lines of a creator who's gradually refined their concept into a fully fleshed-out screenplay.

Formatting

The topic of formatting comes up all the time in the amateur screenwriting world and consumes far too much of people's energy. 99.9% of screenwriting questions can be answered with one simple piece of advice – stop worrying! Stop worrying what people think and strap on a pair.

I get it; internet forums are full of people fretting over this issue and telling others that the slightest formatting error will see your script tossed straight in the trash by a reader. I've literally seen people with zero industry knowledge make that claim. I also know there's plenty of people out there calling themselves script consultants who like to shout from the rooftops about how using too many lines in an action paragraph, the term *"we see"*, or even the odd adverb is screenwriting suicide. This is all little more than paranoia from amateurs and scaremongering from opportunists.

Those who encourage this mania spend their lives parasitically feeding off the desperate need new writers have for approval and are themselves obsessed with the superficial side of scriptwriting because the real subjects of storytelling craft and artistry are beyond their skillset. They like to scare new writers with their dire warnings about formatting errors because it generates clicks and shares. There's also a lot of writers who simply buy into the fear because they want to believe their adherence to these "rules" gives them some sort of advantage over the next person. I can't tell you how many people I've seen on internet forums with barely a few months' experience in screenwriting, absolutely no credentials, no industry contacts, and no direct experience, shouting from the rooftops that everyone must follow rule X, Y, and Z if they want to succeed; otherwise, they are doomed to fail.

On the flip side, I have *never* seen a working screenwriter with verifiable credits tell amateurs they need to fret about their formatting. If anything, I've only seen the opposite. Like all forms of art, people are pretty chill about the form, providing it gets the results.

Example: In 1975, in a small bedroom in the Bronx, New York, twelve-year-old Theodore Livingston was listening to records far too loud when his mother stormed into the room to scold him. In a bid to fall silent and respectfully listen through his mother's lecturing, Theodore broke the cardinal sin when it comes to being a disc jockey – never ever touch the vinyl when it's playing because it will scratch against the needle. By grabbing the record and adjusting it back to where it was before being interrupted, and falling in love with that sound it made in the process, he serendipitously created the first "scratching", a technique he'd go on to perform during his DJ sessions and which would go on to become a fundamental part of turntablism within the revolutionary hip-hop music scene. By doing the very thing he was told not to do, under the belief it would sound awful, the "Grand Wizzard Theodore", as he came to be known, found a sound that would define a generation.

Look, if another writer, consultant, or reader chooses to judge our storytelling abilities on such superficialities of petty formatting rules – rules which more often than not exist only in their own minds – then we owe it to ourselves to turn the other way and run; run as fast as possible away from those people because they are pedants and dullards. Believe me, you do not want to learn from people who think this way. They have got it all backwards. Artistry will always beat out pomposity.

How to Format a Screenplay

- Use screenwriting software (it will do the hard work for you).
- Read a bunch of screenplays to see how much they can vary.
- Use what brings out the best in yourself as a writer and enjoy it.
- Put confidence and enthusiasm on the page.

How Not to Format a Screenplay

Try not to stray too far away from the norms. Our role is to be creative with story and words, not typography and layout. That's it. That's all you need to do.

The "You're Not Freaking Tarantino" Argument

We know the drill. The topic of screenwriting rules is discussed for the 800th time this week on a screenwriter forum and someone brings up how Tarantino gets to write how he wants because he "paid his dues".

Here's the thing – Tarantino never paid his dues before expressing himself as an artist. You know why? Because he's a true artist, and true artists aren't obsessed with trying to box themselves in and fit a mould. Tarantino had his writing rejected over and over, to the point that narrow-minded producers were scrawling abuse on his cover pages before mailing the script back to his agent in disgust. The rejection got to the point that, after finishing his first draft of *Reservoir Dogs*, he told his producer – Lawrence Bender – that if he didn't like it, he'd go shoot it himself in 35mm anyway. Go and read the history books. It's all there.

What Tarantino never did was wimp out when someone disliked his style. Just the same as he didn't wimp out when Tony Scott wanted him to rewrite the ending of *True Romance*. Just the same as he didn't wimp out when the first Sundance Director's Institute panel ripped his directing style to pieces. Just the same as he didn't wimp out when Harvey (Scissor Hands) Weinstein insisted he cut his ear slicing scene if he wanted a distribution deal. Just the same as he didn't wimp out when Oliver Stone, chagrined that Tarantino wouldn't rewrite *Natural Born Killers* for him, sat him down and criticised him for making little movies instead of real films. And, you know what, he didn't wimp out when *Pulp Fiction* was rejected on the grounds of too much violence and poor structure – despite there being a $1m writer-director deal at stake. Tarantino is not a writer who's ever been given permission to do as he wants – he's a writer who has the strength to give himself permission to do what he wants. That's the mindset a true artist adopts, and the results draw in an audience.

And this is the same story over and over for all the writers we admire. They are damn good storytellers who take control of their scripts, making them their domain, because they know it's their job to make the script their domain. What's really needed on the page? Confidence and enthusiasm! Two elements that will be significantly lacking in any writer who's become scared of their own shadow.

Unfilmables & Directing on the Page

So, there's this game I've been playing for years on screenwriting forums. Every now and then, a troll will join the community and start throwing their weight around, often boasting about some ambiguous successes they are having while knocking others down via very basic screenwriting advice. At some point, someone will raise the topic of "unfilmables" in their script, such as a character's thoughts and emotions, and ask if it's okay to do so. As soon as I see this, I'll often post the following and ask for advice on it.

"Those words. The way he said it. She's grabbing her purse, clearing out of the room. Slamming the door behind her. Click. It's locked."

The trolls always fall for it. They can't help themselves. They assume the line is from one of my own scripts and leap at the chance to tell me what an amateurish writer I am and how I will never work in the industry. I then point out this is, in fact, a line from the screenplay *The Bourne Identity* (2002) penned by Edgar Award winner and Academy Award nominee Tony Gilroy; I can then feel their faces turning red through my monitor.

Unfilmables, along with directing on the page, are often contentious subjects where the vast majority of writers will state that you should never do either. This is bad advice when it's presented so sweepingly and conclusively. The reality is, it's actually okay to do this in moderation and in certain ways. In fact, a script will often be better for it, providing it's executed well. Those that say unfilmables are unacceptable, and that a writer should never direct on the page, are also presenting a hypocritical argument. If you want a character to express something internal, then what could be more directorial than writing down specifically how you want them to physically act?

I can state – from talking to veterans in the industry – that many believe nothing pulls in talent like prose that has some wit and soul to it. In fact, I know of at least one A-List actor who decided to sign onto a project in the opening scene of a script because of all the little unfilmable details that made it an entertaining read.

I can also say, from experience, that giving actors what the character is thinking in their head rather than instructions on how to act will work much better for them in building their performance. It makes far more sense to state a character is worried what someone will say next, than trying to describe the complex set of subtle mannerisms a person may show in that situation. Dictating every physical move they make, because you've gotten into this mindset that you can only write prose that details what the camera can see, will only make the actor's job harder when trying to decode what the motivation is behind it all.

You can also hack the problem easily. If the following line, "Jane's worried he's about to fire her", is sacrilegious to the craft, then simply change it to "Jane looks worried he's about to fire her" since this breaks no "rules" as it makes the same statement from a visual context and certainly reads better than "Jane's eyes bulge and nostrils flare a little as she takes a short sharp intake of breath and grips the edge of her desk, the veins on the side of her neck pulsing and sweat forming on her brow". Try giving that to an actor, and see if it helps them give their best performance.

It's also fine to use terms like "we see" and imply significant camera movements or editing tricks if it helps sell the scene just the same, as you are effectively choreographing your cast, dictating wardrobe, and determining locations by simply writing a slug line, character description, or action sequence. There has to be something to work with, and nobody with production experience is reading a script and seeing any of it as permanent. Write with passion and get people excited about your vision.

As ever, there's always a line that can be crossed and knowing where it falls can be subject to many factors. The best thing any aspiring writer can do is read spec scripts that have gotten other previously unknown writers work. That will help you find the balance.

Good prose is simply good prose, and writing something that's vivid and concise with a good flow – while still production-orientated – is an art form in itself. It cannot be dumbed down to "never do this or that".

Industry members are looking for great stories that will make great films, and no sane producer or executive is going to turn their back on a captivating story over something as minor as the writer specifying a transition or camera angle; nor are they going to spend time and money on a script purely because the writer proved they could jump through a certain set of hoops.

Your Voice

Something else you should notice when reading professional scripts is the prominence of a distinct voice and how that can vary radically between different writers.

The term voice applies to writers like style applies to painters or sound applies to musicians. It's something that's all-encompassing and present within every element of the artist's creation at both macro and micro levels but sometimes difficult to define. Voice isn't just tone and turn of phrase, it's expression across the board, including the kind of reoccurring themes the artist finds themselves drawn to, and their philosophical leanings.

> **Example:** Taylor Sheridan, with credits including *Sicario* (2015), *Hell or High Water* (2016), and *Yellowstone* (2008 onward), has become the king of the modern western. His character-driven scripts – which are typically located in the badlands – lack exposition and play thematically in the grey areas of law and morality. They are unmistakably his work thanks to his distinctive artistic voice within a well-established genre.

As you write more and more, and become increasingly comfortable with storytelling, you should see your own voice start to emerge as you express yourself more freely. My recommendation is that you own it and lean into it. Do not run from who you are artistically, especially if you think others will be put off by it. There is room for every voice, and the more diverse out there, the better. There will be something unique you bring to the table, and not only is that valuable to others, but it's also where your purpose most likely lies as a creative. You probably didn't get into this to blend into the background – at least I hope you didn't – so be proud of what makes you you.

If you have the opposite problem and your scripts feel dull because they lack any kind of voice, consider adopting the imitation hack I wrote about in the dialogue section, but apply it to your prose. Write your script as you would imagine one of your heroes writing the same script. It sounds crazy, but it can work. Sometimes, it's easier to give ourselves permission to let loose and express ourselves confidently when we're doing it seemingly through a proxy. If you love the work of James Gunn or James Cameron, then approach your script as if you're in their heads and do what you think they would do. Of course, you aren't these individuals and shouldn't try to be them, but adopting their mindset might just give you the confidence needed to allow your own voice to flourish.

Software

As mentioned earlier, you need to be using screenwriting software, and there's no excuse not to. The automatic formatting will make your life a lot easier, and it will generate the professional looking PDF file needed to circulate your script along with the industry-standard working file should it ever go into development. Given that there are free options out there for every platform, you're gaining nothing by using clunky Word or Google Docs templates which will only likely make your life harder.

So, what's the best screenwriting software out there? You're going to get a lot of people, mainly amateurs, telling you that you need to be using Final Draft, that it's the industry-standard, and the best there is. Please consider the following:

- Neil Cross (*Spooks, Dr Who, Luther*) uses Scrivener.
- Craig Mazin (*The Hangover Pt2 & 3, Identity Thief, Chernobyl*) uses Fade In.
- Phil Lord (*Spider-Man: Into the Spider-Verse, The Lego Movie, 21 & 22 Jump Street*) uses Highland 2.
- Ted Elliott & Terry Rossio (*Pirates of the Caribbean, Shrek, Aladdin*) use Movie Magic Screenwriter.
- Scott Stewart (*Legion, Dark Skies, Dominion*) uses Slugline.
- Christopher Ford (*Robot & Frank, Spider-Man: Homecoming*) uses Writer Duet.

So, based on all that evidence, don't tell me Final Draft is the best piece of screenwriting software out there and the first choice for all Hollywood professionals.

A lot of people push others into buying Final Draft since the proprietary XML derived file format it uses (.FDX) is an industry standard that plugs into many other production and scheduling programs. However, there is no industry standard for writing stories, and pretty much everything out there can output perfectly in FDX format. Therefore, no writer should fear they may choose the wrong software to work with. Plus, it takes about five minutes to pick up and learn a new program. Seriously, there's nothing to fear. People make way too big a deal about this. I don't have any beef with Final Draft per se, it's a great bit of software, but I do have a beef with artists being told *which tools to use*.

The best screenwriting software choice is whatever brings out the best in you as an individual and, given that screenwriting software is so easy to pick up and use, you really owe it to yourself to experiment with what's out there.

When do you need Final Draft? The moment you go pro is the time you absolutely should have it installed, as you'll most likely be making revisions back and forth with a producer and potentially doing rewrites on set. You can download a demo and get familiar with it beforehand, but it's far from complicated to get to grips with. You can also get the Final Draft app for your phone/tablet, allowing you to open and edit files on the road. For what it's worth, I did onset rewrites for a film on an iPad using the Final Draft app, and it got the job done.

Personally, I develop and draft in Scrivener because I love the way all project files are broken down into smaller documents (aka "scrivens"). Thus, not only can I have all my development docs within that project file, I can break down my script into acts, sequences, and scenes, and focus only on what I need to, along with having specific notes and snapshots for those scenes. Scrivener was developed by writers for writers, and it really shows as it's an excellent composition tool. Like all good screenwriting software, it exports in .FDX as well, so when my first draft is done, and I'm making tweaks with a producer or director, I can simply shift across to Final Draft and start using revision mode as we collaborate.

I also really like the look of Writer Duet and Highland 2 as a couple of alternatives. The former is feature-heavy and runs in a browser, meaning it can run on something as cheap as a Chromebook, while the latter is beautifully clean and minimalist in its interface, making composition as pleasant as possible. Plus, as mentioned previously, I'm also a big fan of Prewrite, which is designed to make developing your story as easy as possible before moving on to drafting.

When I first got into screenwriting, there were only half a dozen software options, whereas there are now easily over twenty programs worth considering. Most have demos. Try them. You have nothing to lose. Even if it only makes you love your first choice more, at least you know you made the right choice and can find peace with that. Don't worry about what anybody else thinks and don't think you have to spend much money. You can write just as good a script on a $200 laptop running free software as the next person with a $1,500 MacBook and the latest copy of Final Draft.

My Mistakes with Drafting

Like many new writers, I wrote my first script using software I was most familiar with and had installed on my computer – Microsoft Word! I decided I didn't want to spend money on a new program and got hold of a free template I found online, which had all the margins and fonts set correctly, along with style options to switch between all the common elements. Like many new writers who go this route, I also spent pretty much the entire script clumsily switching elements and stopping in my tracks every twenty minutes to check if I was formatting things correctly.

On the one side, I was simply so excited to be creating something that looked like a script. It seemed so official and professional. On the other side, I was constantly worried that I was failing to format this official and professional-looking document correctly and had to keep looking up what I could on the Internet. Plus, as the document got longer, it became increasingly unwieldy to work with, stuttering as I tried to scroll through it with no easy way to jump straight to scenes and make changes.

I didn't realise – at the time – that I was making my own life so much harder by using a piece of software that wasn't designed with screenwriting in mind, and I was making myself paranoid by reading various script formatting guides online. Those guides were full of dogmatic rules that made presenting a script feel like going on military parade, and worse still, no two seemed to agree fully with each other on which way was the correct way. Programming in code felt less strict in comparison. "Never go above four action lines!", "Your script should be X pages long!", "If you ever use 'we see' your script will be thrown out!", "If you direct on the page, people will think you're a control freak!", "Bold slug-lines? Syd Field himself will visit you in the night and break both your legs!". It was all highly intimidating, and the information was presented as rules that would make or break ever being allowed into the Hollywood fold. What's more, it was plaguing my mind with more and more fear when I wrote, and making the process considerably less enjoyable.

I think it was about six months into writing when I finally committed to springing a little cash on some dedicated screenwriting software and wow! That first time using the tab key to switch elements from slug to action to dialogue, plus the benefit of the autocomplete feature on character names, it was like my first time driving a car with an automatic transmission. It was so much easier, and it freed up my mind so I could focus on what mattered – the writing!

I'd fallen into the trap of seeing writing as primitive, and with such a low barrier to entry, it wasn't worth investing in when it came to tools. I was wrong to think like that. Writing software to a writer is like an instrument to a musician. The responsiveness matters. The composing window matters. The impact on the eyes matters. The same goes for the keyboard, mouse, and monitor. This is the coalface we spend our time slowly chiselling away at. We have to find that place as comfortable, welcoming, and empowering as possible.

When it came to formatting, I eventually closed the reductive guides down and opened up PDFs of produced scripts instead to study them. That was enlightening. I saw just how flexible those supposed rules were and how varied scripts could be; some were flowery and detailed while others were staccato and to the point. What was abundant was confidence and charisma on the page with highly distinctive voices that often felt informal and witty. These writers had clearly taken control of their domain. It was their show, and they were determined to make the read vivid and entertaining.

One script that had really caught my attention and affection was *The Bourne Identity* by Tony Gilroy, an unusually formatted script that uses lots of double-dashes -- and short -- broken up -- sentences. I loved it. It was the first time I really saw a writer's voice shine, and I imitated the style in my next script. Despite the fundamental formatting of the prose being so unusual, I never got any complaints about it and Amazon Studios – who were taking amateur submissions via their website at the time – showcased my script out of ten thousand others. And I'm pretty sure they didn't suspect it was Tony Gilroy writing under a pseudonym! A fearless attitude had really paid off.

Screenplay formatting is so simple, and now so automated, I think people have to try to overcomplicate it to have something to say. I also think that people, particularly those who did well within the academic system, enter screenwriting with a similar mindset where their ability to comply and fit in will go a long way toward the "grade" they'll get in the reader's mind. You combine these two, and you've got people who love to make up rules and others who love to hear about them.

Something I did struggle with for years, particularly as I learned more about the craft, was my mind being in two places as I wrote. I was trying to be as ingrained into the moment as possible but had a lot of nagging thoughts about structure and page count going on in the background. I also strongly disliked rewriting as any semblance of logic behind my words would quickly dissolve into a soup. Like many creatives, I do not have an ordered mind. I'm at the mercy of a chaotic lump of electrified meat full of daydreams, abstraction, and anxiety. The idea of breaking down a script and rewriting it felt akin to deciphering one of Einstein's equations and improving it.

The solution was to embrace pre-writing, which I wish had been spoken about more, so I'd perhaps learned about it earlier. In my case, it came about organically from my increasingly detailed development process. I was already structuring my acts, putting together a treatment, and breaking down my scenes. Why wouldn't I just take all those points, transfer them into a script document, and build outward from them? Why would I want to take a tentative stab in the dark by going in blind, all while knowing I will have to digest what I've done and come back for another go over and over again until it feels right? That seems terribly inefficient and, to this day, I can't understand why so many writers choose to work this way. You're on draft seven? Okay, so you've wasted your time getting it wrong at least six times already?

The more I pre-wrote, the less I rewrote, and hours spent preparing at the start saved days fixing at the end. I felt empowered, liberated, and like a true artist, honing my work out of something fleshed out and able to focus 100% on the moment I was writing – without any doubt or worry I was drifting off course. While I tightened up my overly descriptive action lines and timed my action scenes to run to one page per minute, I showed a lot more confidence on the page and made the document mine. This was my shot at telling the best version I could of my story. I found my voice and I built on it, leaning into it rather than being ashamed of it, and my scripts became tighter, better-crafted, and stronger as a result.

These days, my scripts – particularly my spec scripts – have a distinct style I'm very proud of. With my illustrated cover pages, bold slug-lines, unfilmable beats, and titled chapters, I'm certainly breaking the rules by some people's standards and pushing the boundaries by most. My stance is take it or leave it. I'm not interested in creating art with academics, analysts, and accountants. I've learned that this industry, and the audience that it serves, loves rebels, and I've learned to embrace being one.

A problem I've never run into and want to make note of is writer's block. I feel writer's block only exists if you believe in it and making that mistake gives your mind the excuse it needs to hold back and procrastinate. It's critical to let go of the concept that creativity flows from us in an inspired fashion. Sometimes, it needs teasing or even dragging out of us, and a great way to do that is by pre-writing, which should ask us the questions we need to ask ourselves, get any ideas out of our minds onto paper, and allow us to indulge in the areas that most motivate us at the time. There's plenty of times I've needed prompting, and never a time has that prompting failed to trigger new ideas.

If you've read this far, I should have given you more than enough, by now, to jump in and write a well-structured script from start to finish. In the next chapter, we'll talk about career building, in which your approach and attitude will have a significant impact on your artistic development.

CHAPTER 7: CAREER BUILDING

As if mastering the black art of screenwriting wasn't enough, trying to get a script *produced* is an even more mysterious world fraught with danger.

There's basically one rule that rings true; nobody knows anything.

That applies to each one of us all the way up to the top players in Hollywood. Seriously, just read up on how some of the best movies ever made only did so after streams of rejections from decision-makers. The popular writers out there haven't succeeded because of the way the industry works; they've succeeded *despite* the way the industry works. Keep this in mind whenever you get a pass or negative feedback.

** I couldn't get past the readers at studios. The minute people actually in the studios who read boring scripts all the time actually read my shit, they were like, 'This shit is awesome! Send it right to us!' but the readers would never let it get there. **/

Quentin Tarantino, while interviewed on the Howard Stern show

The reality of a screenwriting career is so elusive the term is bordering on an oxymoron. Most amateur writers give up before ever breaking in. Over 50% of WGA writers do not go on to earn a dime after their first success. Everyone struggling up the greasy pole reports the same experience – the further you advance, the harder it gets.

It doesn't help that the world's focus is set firmly on Hollywood, where the film industry is run with the kind of politics found in a high school cheerleader squad blended with the kind of business ethics of a Victorian workhouse. The result is something daunting on the whole, with faint glimmers of opportunity in the cracks. Sure, there seem to be screenwriters out there living the dream, but they are minuscule blades of hay in a mountain of needles.

What matters above all is our personal integrity; are we presenting the scripts we want to write? I've seen too many writers get sucked into the 'get feedback and try to please everyone void' in a bid to sell scripts, and I've skated around the outside of it myself. It's a sure way to become a writer who desperately churns out redrafted material like it's high school coursework, all the while trying to hit some mystical marking criteria. We are not school kids, we are not worker bees, we are artists; we must act as such and have the guts to respect our gut, as convoluted and twisted it may be.

So how are we, as aspiring creatives, to move forward?

It Isn't About Fitting In; It's About Finding Your Fit

With most recent generations before us working single-track careers, we've become predisposed to the concept of a job for life. The result of this is an attitude of keeping our nose to the grindstone from nine to five and asking "*how high*" when we're told to jump by our superiors.

There's something uncomfortably servile about the way many try to lean into a screenwriting career, especially when considering how corporate values are so poorly aligned with the common mindset of a creative. In fact, it might be fair to say creativity and industrialisation are fundamentally opposed; each will only ever frustrate the other.

But times are changing fast as millions of workers walk out of the full-time lifestyle and choose a more fulfilling path. In my case, my own career is oddball and I'm thankful for that. I was working freelance for a household name while still at high school. I skipped university and went straight into a well-paid job after leaving school. I had my own office by 19, and I was a company director before I turned 25, plus I've dipped in and out of self-employment like there's nothing to fear during all those years.

I've had it tough, too.

In contrast to that affluence, I've also spent nearly a decade earning less than minimum wage and struggling to get by (to the point where I've had to consider living in my car). I've had a lot, and I've lost a lot. It's only because of those experiences that I have maintained the self-confidence to pursue *what I want* rather than live with what I'm given. We are only now becoming empowered to live by our own rules. However, as a majority, it's taking us a long time to adjust.

Something I've come to learn – and I think it's sadly something many of us are oblivious to – is that a fulfilling working life is all about orientating our environments to suit our needs, rather than trying to manipulate ourselves to suit our environments. We are, ultimately, irrational emotional beings and we benefit more from reflecting on that, than we do trying to ignore or rationalise it.

It's really up to us to better understand ourselves and approach the industry with this understanding. Many of us grumble we're in the wrong job, but whose fault is that? We have to accept it might be ours. It's not always the case that our work sucks, or our boss sucks. It's often the case that we're simply in a dysfunctional working relationship.

Maybe you're the type of person who wants a single-track career. There's nothing wrong with that. Maybe you're the kind of person who wants a portfolio career. There's nothing wrong with that either. What is wrong is complaining the hole is round without realising we're a square peg. And, no, aversion to risk is never a good excuse not to follow the right path to fulfilment. Surely it makes sense to compromise the material things in life in the short-term rather than our own wellbeing over the long-term, right?

For many of us, writing doesn't have to be a full-time job for life. It may not even need to be a career switch. Writing can be part-time. It can be unpaid. It can be a hobby. It can be *whatever we choose it to be*. The writers to envy are the ones who've found the right balance for them. We need to be wary we don't get caught up in the aspirations of others for fear we resent a situation that's actually good for us.

Learn From Success, Not Failure

Screenwriting communities are obsessed with the concept that learning from failure is the route to self-improvement. While I do like the notion that we should never fear failure, this whole concept runs into some serious issues within the context of subjectivity. You see, if we are tasked with the job of designing a bridge and – after being built to our design – that bridge falls down, we have without doubt failed. However, someone passing on our scripts, someone not liking our work, someone hating our material – all this is not necessarily failure on our part. We cannot be held accountable for the tastes and expectations of others any more than we can be held accountable for picking the wrong PowerBall numbers for the draw next weekend.

Worse still, this is a highly demotivating attitude to adopt as a writer. It's only likely that our work will be seen as imperfect by some, maybe even hated, and thinking that issue can be addressed time after time is a route to madness, not improvement. There is going to be a point where many of us burn out because we end up going in circles trying to please everyone.

Focussing on our successes proves to ourselves the reality of subjectivity and motivates us to progress further. Simply starting that first script is a huge success and proof our ambitions can become actions. Finishing that script is another huge success and proof we can put the work in. Studying craft is a success. Redrafting is a success. Sharing our scripts is, too, and – here's the thing – having anyone appreciate what we are doing, be it only in a tiny way, is a massive success. Does this mean ignoring our weaknesses? Certainly not. Objective craft development and a high standard of professionalism are essential but also a lot easier to tackle with a good dose of self-confidence.

We can either build on what we know has worked for us, or we can obsess over what hasn't; two very different ways of looking at the same problem. The former reinforces the belief we have in ourselves, motivates us to write in the way we love to write, and assures us the future is all a matter of serendipity. The latter slowly strips away our self-confidence, homogenises our voice into something mediocre, and causes us to falsely believe we'll fail until we fit in. Let's give ourselves permission to see ourselves as ongoing success stories *now*, rather than hope we'll be seen as such in the future.

The Danger of the Cinderella Narrative

If you've never heard of the Cinderella Narrative, then good; it's a term I invented myself, and I'm totally going to copyright it one day. I find many who want to succeed in the entertainment industry suffer from this deluded pattern of thinking. People seem to think that, if they just keep their heads down and work, whilst fantasising about their wildest dreams coming true, and making sure everyone knows they don't really expect those dreams to happen, a fairy godmother is going to eventually materialise out of nowhere, applaud them for their remarkable humility, and whisk them into the limelight where their true talents will finally be admired by all, opening the floodgates to fame, glamour, and fortune. They'll sweep the floors obediently and sing to the mice quietly until they're catapulted into the royal ball and proposed to by Prince Charming.

Life isn't a Disney movie, and sadly, as I expressed in the first chapter, stories teach us about life and not always in a healthy way. The world is full of ageing princesses who can't understand why – after years of being meek and persevering – their pumpkin carriage has yet to roll up outside and take them to the castle to be universally adored.

The narrative of Cinderella, at least in its more modernised form, is a paradoxical one, the paradox being that, if you believe you will be rewarded for showing humility, how can that humility ever be taken as genuine in the first place? What Cinderella subconsciously teaches many is how to hack karma for selfish gain. We've all met those people who can't wait to tell us how much they despise the idea of being famous, and have no use for money, yet always linger in the spotlight until they outstay their welcome and already have their perfect Aston Martin configured and costed. Sadly, modesty is all too often driven by ego.

With aspiring writers, this adoption of the Cinderella Narrative tends to manifest itself in keeping scripts pretty much locked away while writing diligently and being resistant to any kind of self-promotion while growing increasingly frustrated at having not been "discovered" by Hollywood and not had a red carpet rolled out that leads straight up to the podium on the Oscars stage.

It doesn't help that success often looks like this from the outside in, even though we're constantly reminded it often takes decades to become an overnight sensation, and it certainly doesn't help that there are those one-in-million cases where someone quietly working in a corner suddenly becomes a huge success.

Example: Starting in July 2003 and inspired by a dream she had one night, Stephanie Meyer wrote a vampire romance novel in secret and with no intention to publish it until her sister persuaded her to send it out to agencies. One showed interest in this manuscript named *Twilight* and held an auction for the rights between eight publishers, resulting in Meyer signing a $750K three-book deal only six months after typing the first words. Five years later, in 2008, she was earning in excess of $50m per year.

Also in 2003, Brook Busey adopted the pen-name Diablo Cody and started writing a blog named *The Pussy Ranch*, which detailed her adventures working as a stripper. The blog went viral and drew the attention of a manager who secured her a book deal and encouraged her to try writing a screenplay. In 2008, following the release of *Juno*, Cody received the Academy Award for Best Original Screenplay. None of this is in the slightest bit normal.

The reality for most, when it comes to building a career, is that it's a long, arduous journey in which you have to be proactive and comfortable with promoting yourself as often and in as many ways as possible. If you aren't giving it at least ten years to break in, while working hard at it, you aren't giving your dream enough time to manifest.

"Breaking in" is the term used by people within the film industry to describe going from an amateur to a working professional. The fact it's described akin to having to smash through a seemingly impenetrable wall says a lot about how tough it's considered to be, and how rare breaking through actually is.

The good news is there's a general phenomenon that suggests the longer it takes to build something up, the longer it takes to break something down. Genuine overnight success has a habit of flaming out very quickly and defining an artist by a tiny sample of material that pigeon-holes them and holds them to continuing the same level of success – with the same type of content – for fear of appearing to fail. Try to see your ongoing advancement upward as smoothing out the fall downward, after you inevitably peak.

The harsh truth is that anyone who believes screenwriting is a route to seeing their name in lights, walking the red carpet, being on the front page of magazines, mingling with stars, receiving awards, or a way to make big money fast is writing for all the wrong reasons, and most likely going to find the results frustrating and disappointing. Those of us who get to sit in a warm room on our own time, expressing ourselves via the written word, are incredibly privileged. Those of us who get to share a journey with like-minded creatives, and maybe do something that makes the world a slightly better place by bringing a new film into it, have hit the jackpot in life.

Waiting for the Cavalry

Tied to the Fairy Godmother element above, and another form of naive bad-think, is the ongoing belief that some form of cavalry is going to arrive at some point and carry you triumphantly into the inner circles of Hollywood where you quickly get comfortable and have a career for life. This usually manifests itself as an obsession with getting an agent but also extends to winning screenwriting competitions and having a break-out film.

The film industry is less like a cavalry and more like a travelling circus; picking people up along the way in the hope they can either pull ropes or entertain a paying audience and leaving them behind should they fail to do either. It is cold, ruthless, frighteningly short-sighted, and happy to move on tomorrow at full-steam regardless of who's missing.

Representation in the form of agents and managers isn't what it's often made out to be. There's no slingshot into Tinsel Town. Yes, there are some powerful individuals out there who keep their clients busy, well-compensated, and feeling valued, but they represent the top 1% in their field and don't go scouting for unknown talent.

The remaining 99% are often inactive, uninspired, and apathetic.

In the case of agents, they can sometimes be outright destructive to a client's career and live up to the old joke that they are typically *"arsonists disguised as firefighters"*, something I can confirm as someone who's both watched writers sign with agencies and go nowhere, and also dealt with those agencies from the other side as a producer trying to secure talent.

There's a rule of thumb that can be applied here: you don't need an agent until people can't believe you don't already have one. Getting down to brass tacks, this means you have to be prepared to be your own agent and manager for a significant period of time. You can't sit waiting in the wilderness for someone to come rescue you. You gotta find your inner Andy McNab or Bear Grylls and escape the jungle by your own means in the form of doing your own networking and managing your own career path until people are knocking your door down to work with you. That means getting over any fear of cold-contacting, querying, and relationship building while embracing networking, marketing, and press relations.

Rather than waiting for the cavalry, it makes sense to wait for what feels more like a wave in the form of a win or series of wins, which carry you some way toward the shore before petering out. There will be big waves and small waves, and the time between them could be long or brief. The important thing is to wait patiently for one to build and ride it as long as you can, preferably with little concern for the fickle waters others are swimming in that might sweep them ahead before you.

It's No Longer the Nineties

Like any industry, the film industry goes through significant phases of systemic change that revolutionise how it operates. In the 70s, Hollywood saw the American New Wave, where relatively young auteur directors reclaimed control of film production from studios and took mainstream cinema in a hedonistic new direction which eventually culminated in the form of the modern-day blockbuster.

This repeated itself, to some degree, in the 90s with the Independent Cinema Movement, which took place more so on the small screen than the big one. Videotapes, and later DVDs, created long-tail returns that meant even the most cultish of films had the potential to make theatrical levels of profit that paid in year after year. The result was studios green-lighting diverse "slates" (their varied collections of film projects in development), and they allowed rebellious new directors to do their own thing on the backlots while independent production companies sprouted up wherever an empty office and an unused phone line could be found. This was a golden era for screenwriters as Hollywood was crying out for good spec scripts, the hottest of which would filter through highly proactive agencies such as CAA and find themselves in bidding wars that would sometimes net seven-figure sales for previously unknown writers. This high valuation of writing talent raised the tide for all boats, too, meaning WGA rates were easily within reach for the average working screenwriter outside the studio system. Good times!

However, thirty years on, a lot has changed. Those home video sales have all but dried up, and while not only are the movie theatres now dominated by blockbuster releases throughout the entire year, those blockbusters themselves have to compete in a marketplace saturated by noise.

A movie release isn't the biggest thing happening in the world of pop culture anymore, not for the average customer anyway, who's being bombarded by marketing activities for TV, computer games, apps, events, and much more. Compounding this change in demand is a change in supply. Gone are the times when writers needed a typewriter, the money and time to print and mail scripts, along with the addresses and phone numbers of industry contacts to send them to. Thanks to computing and the internet, the barrier to entry into the world of screenwriting is pretty much resting on the ground. I know a studio executive who believes the industry as a whole has access to maybe as many as 100,000 professional-level screenwriters at any time. These are individuals an industry member can call upon and trust to put together a feature, many of whom are willing to work for very little (even nothing), and many of whom are willing and able to turn work around fast (even overnight). This is quite possibly one of the most competitive professions in the world.

The problem is, many aspiring screenwriters are still living in an age where the $1,000,000 spec sale is commonplace, and this creates a lottery mentality to building a career. Eight out of ten amateur screenwriters seem to be holding out for their numbers to come in and, well, while examples like Evan Daugherty selling his *Snow White and the Huntsman* spec to Universal for $3.2m do exist, they are incredibly unusual and represent the tiny pinnacle of the industry.

A Living Wage Is a Blessing

This is the blunt truth about screenwriting as a profession. Being able to turn it into a career and put food on the table is a rare privilege. The sooner you accept this, the better, as it will adjust your perception of career-building into something more realistic and sustainable while still keeping the door open to that once in a lifetime opportunity.

Very few screenwriters achieve a sale or get an assignment, and even fewer of them go on to have a second success story. Many who do sell rarely receive over five figures for their hard work, and many others only ever see income in the form of option fees on their material – if they're lucky enough to get any option fee at all. It's brutal.

On the flipside, I can tell you that earning a wage that puts a roof over your head and food on your table from writing scripts is a wonderful way to live. You get to do something you love in an industry most people find fascinating. You get to sit in a comfy chair daydreaming for a living while so many others slave away, often physically, at something they hate. Yes, you might have to live in a studio apartment and drive a beat-up old car, but that's the life of an artist. As mentioned previously, there was a time when even Picasso himself had to sketch for this supper.

I know a few "lifers" in the independent scene world who've had to scrape by for most years and had a few big wins that have evened everything out. One of them has a great saying when times get tough; "There's a hell of a lot of people I wouldn't want to switch places with and a tiny few I would."

I've also watched a lot of amateur writers obsess with the thought of a huge studio-level sale, and refuse to accept anything less for over a decade. Even if they sold a script for $100,000 tomorrow, they would still have earned less than the writers I know of who sell one script a year (on average) to small TV networks. Having a few movies of the week may not be seen as making it in the business by many, but it can certainly be lucrative over time and keep a working screenwriter in the game.

Networking is Everything

Look, we can talk about competitions, pitching, querying, evaluations, and ranking services until we're blue in the face, but almost every working filmmaker will tell you that they owe their career to meeting the right person at the right time and, the more people you interact with, the more likely serendipity is going to take place.

Learning to network effectively is daunting but, if you approach it with the right mindset, it can be highly enjoyable.

My top tips are:
- First and foremost, be *yourself*.
- Be upfront and honest about your values and goals.
- Genuinely listen to what people have to say.

- Try to help others solve *their* problems.
- Put pursuing friendship before everything else.

Try to avoid:
- Spamming people en masse with generic messages.
- Monologing about yourself and your projects.
- Asking busy people for time-consuming favours.
- Sending long, drawn-out introductions/correspondences.
- Pressuring people to read material they haven't asked to read.

The aim is to build relationships and not just connections. Genuine friendship and, more to the point, devout loyalty is one of the rarest things to find in filmmaking. The industry member you hope can make things happen for you has most likely had dozen upon dozen aspiring screenwriters pick them up and drop them in an attempt to climb onto their shoulders and get to the next person. People are predatory, ruthless, and creepy in their pursuit of fame and fortune.

To be absolutely blunt about it, and based on personal experience as someone who can get films made, if you aren't a self-serving weirdo, you are already ahead of 90% of your peers. You have nothing to be worried about. Be yourself, know your craft, know the history of the industry, and know the stories behind the films you love. People will want you in their circle and will entertain the idea of working with you.

Keep in mind that you can network both online and in-person, with the former being easier but the latter being more powerful. Websites like LinkedIn and Stage 32 are great, and events like meetups at film festivals or screenings are good too. Again, go for the drinks and conversation and stay for the friendships you make. Don't talk shop, don't pester, and absolutely don't wax-lyrical about your dreams and aspirations like you're the main character in everyone's life.

And you know what? Don't attack Hollywood and other people's films either. Bitterness isn't attractive, and you might just beat down something the person you're conversing with has played a part in.

On top of that, don't segue into what's effectively stalking. I wish I was joking, but I've seen aspiring writers go as far as to recommend getting onto sets to try to sit next to actors during lunch, hanging out by elevators to corner executives in buildings, joining the same dentists as producers to try to get their contact details, and even attending AA meetings in the hope of bumping into industry members at their lowest and most vulnerable. Gross.

ScriptRevolution.com is a platform I put together that represents my best attempt at making networking between writers and filmmakers as easy as possible. It offers a place that hosts scripts for free and allows all filmmakers to browse through them. However, this is only a baseline, and there to be an extension of our overall networking effort – not to replace it. It will only work best for those who treat it professionally.

When you can't network actively, network passively. That means putting yourself out there in some form, so others can discover you and learn more about what you have to offer. Blogging, vlogging, and article writing, in general, are all effectively networking tools that can show how serious you are about the craft, how capable you are of delivering, and how undiscovered you are as an artist. Writing is our domain, so being able to write captivating content that links back to a professionally written bio (you do have a bio, right?) should be a walk in a park for us and become even more powerful if it all connects up and sends readers to our loglines or even our scripts. Now that's thinking like a marketeer!

What absolutely isn't going to work is sheltering yourself away in a dark corner of the internet on some forum, spewing out a monologue of status updates to a few followers on social media, or trying a hard sell in a casual situation – three things I see aspiring writers doing *all the time*. Ultimately, the world is not going to come to you. You have to be prepared to – at least – meet it halfway.

The Marketplace and You as a Product

There are a set of industry forces in place that are inescapable, and you have to view them and yourself with the sense of an entrepreneur. Entering the filmmaking world, unless taking a desk job within a highly corporatised studio or within a well-established writers' room, is essentially the domain of the freelancer. It is nothing like building a typical corporate career.

While the term "hustle" has become overused and over-romanticised of late, it's always going to be a big part of cutting a path into the industry. You need to be your own manager, boss, accountant, marketer, public relations officer, editor, proofreader, lawyer, assistant, and a whole lot more to some extent, particularly in the early days. Therefore, you must understand the market, how it operates, and how you fit into it as a supplier.

You effectively have two offerings: your voice and your concepts. Your voice, as mentioned earlier, is what makes your writing uniquely yours. Having a strong voice means your fingerprints should be all over your material. This is highly subjective in terms of appeal and can be polarising. It's also what you'll be least known for (at first) due to very few people having read your scripts or seen any films made from them.

Your concepts, on the other hand, will have objective appeal regardless of your lack of prominence within the industry since the entire premise behind your story has intrinsic value. If your concept features an intriguing plot hook or suggests the script contains content that's in demand, industry members are going to see potential ticket sales before they've even turned a page.

For example, having a zombie- or vampire-based spec script in 2010 meant you had the type of content that production companies were actively seeking out due to consumer demand. Westerns, on the other hand, were going straight to the bottom of the slush pile following a string of high-profile failures.

However, there are significant hurdles to overcome. In the case of voice and craft skills, a new writer lacks any benefit of the doubt. This is critical and the main stumbling block that all artists suffer from when relatively unknown within an industry. Most industry members are trying to triage an unstoppable influx of material and looking for excuses NOT to read through another hundred pages of low-effort garbage. A cold query from a writer with no credentials is an understandably good enough reason to give a quick pass and focus on the people who've been recommended by peers, endorsed by trusted sources, and already shown to be working.

When it comes to concepts, the hurdle is timing the marketplace, which is something even Hollywood itself fails to do with its releases. The subject of whether or not a screenwriter can realistically write for the market could fill a book in itself, but it's fair to say a genuinely intriguing premise will always have high appeal, and there are certain elements that are consistently in demand. (It can certainly pay to have a glamorous and sexy feeling low-budget action-thriller that lacks strong violence and profanity, has a sense of humour, and doesn't require excessive stunts and SFX to make a reality.) Go tour the discount DVD bin of your local grocery store to get a sense of the kind of film everyone feels stands the greatest chance of turning a profit. Is the industry unimaginative, risk-averse, and short-sighted? Yes. But industries tend to be, and fighting against it when you're a nobody is futile.

Therefore, the vast majority of your successes will be down to people valuing your artistic voice as they become familiar with you and/or the commercial appeal of your story concepts at any given time. This is what I call *"alignment"*, and it drives everything.

It's All About Alignment

If there's one concept I want you to walk away with, after reading this chapter, it's the concept of alignment driving career success.

Alignment is when *what you have to offer* as a writer *matches what industry members are looking for.* This sounds obvious, but I feel most writers trying to break in refuse to accept it's the fundamental driving force behind any form of creative arts. You cannot get around a failure of alignment and should not let it cause you to think there's anything lacking on your side of the equation. Most passes, in my opinion, are mainly due to a lack of alignment – the writer simply has something that's conceptually, tonally, and/or logistically undesirable to the reader. It's rarely about execution because a script that has a lot of potential is easily rewritten to maximise that potential.

If you read up on the life stories of your filmmaking heroes, particularly cult heroes, you'll likely see how they battled with a lack of alignment for years or even decades until they met the right person. What they most likely didn't do was give up on their vision, question their artistic voice, and start butchering their material to please their detractors during the interim; if they did, the results were probably disastrous.

Try to think of it like this: reflect on all those times you've watched films with friends, and how often you've loved films others have hated and vice-versa. Now think about how often the person who disliked a film – including perhaps yourself – felt like it was a bad film with objective issues such as poor production value, plot holes, poor casting, weak performances, clunky writing, flat lighting, bad costume design, etc. Maybe a film your friend thought was whimsical, you found pretentious. Perhaps a film you loved for its hedonism a friend called dumb.

I once showed a couple *Black Dynamite* (2009), a comedy spoof of old blaxsploitation movies, and while the husband immediately ordered a Blu-ray copy for himself because he found it so hilarious, his wife was borderline angry at how terrible she thought it was (at every level). She didn't realise that many of her complaints were actually a deliberate effort by the filmmakers, since they were making a parody; the film failed to align with her and she lost interest and focus early on. The same is happening with your scripts whenever they're read. Those who simply don't like your material, and were probably never going to enjoy it in the first place, will often attempt to justify their emotional response by coming up with technical flaws that may exist only in their head.

To some extent, it's worth looking at alignment like dating; your voice is your personality and your concepts represent your objective attractiveness to people in general. You're going to have a hard time pairing up with someone who doesn't like beards if you have facial hair fit for a pirate and, the more popular you already are, the less effort you're going to have to put in to get people to know you. And much like dating, the more desperate people are for a match, the more welcoming people are to the idea that the other party can grow into something more appealing. Long story short, industry members who are hungry for material are going to be looking at your script with a very open mind as to how it can be changed to suit their needs. It's just words on a page, after all.

That means there's hope, particularly in the low-budget indie world, but only if you're willing to adapt to other people's wishes. The big studios, acclaimed production companies, and known directors, however… well, they have a lot of suiters and every right to be fussy about who they let into their worlds.

The Mythical Bastard Reader God

While it's well known that studios, production companies, and industry members employ the services of readers to filter through submissions, there is a lot of demonisation and reverence over their role. Many writers seem to feel production company readers are there to be both simultaneously worshipped and hated. There are just as many bad readers out there as there are writers.

I know of highly opinionated readers who judge a script by the cover page, freak out over formatting, and love dishing out "tough love" (i.e., are sociopathic slush trolls in love with their own opinion). I also know of some incredible readers who are genuinely giving every script the benefit of the doubt and looking for the potential that even the original writer may fail to see. They are humans and, more often than not, failed writers.

In summary, some readers are complete douchebags, some are saints, and most fall somewhere in the middle. Just keep in mind that a professionally-employed reader will be expected to read submitted scripts from beginning to end, so stop listening to people who say scripts get thrown in the trash the second the reader spots a spelling mistake or isn't kept as continually excited as a dog watching their owner put walking shoes on.

But while readers aren't gods, they are gatekeepers nonetheless, and that has to be appreciated. Year after year sees wave after wave of new writers throwing brand new material down every avenue they can, to get noticed. The industry has every reason to impose cold, harsh filtering, and every excuse to miss the diamonds in the rough.

Again, alignment plays a big part in moving up the system by getting a *consider* or a *recommend* from a reader with the caveat that most readers don't have as much awareness of the market or experience with logistics as the producers and execs they work for. They are generally going to favour good storytelling craft above all else.

Ideally, you want fewer steps between you and the producer or executive who's the key decision-maker, so you're reducing the chances of someone failing to align with your work and killing its progress upward with a pass. To do that, you need to form relationships with those decision-makers and get them excited about what your work can do for them, so they read it (and judge it) themselves.

What you don't want to do – and which many people make the mistake of doing – is to start writing to please readers and thus become afraid of putting off anybody over the slightest of controversial choices. This will almost certainly result in weakening your voice, your most valuable asset, as you buy into the collective paranoia of screenwriting communities and the collections of Chinese whispers they like to call rules.

The Ugly Topic of Compensation

Knowing how much you should be getting paid to write, or even if you should be getting paid at all, is a hotly debated topic between writers trying to break in. It's a topic that many people are never going to see eye-to-eye on.

There are two forces at work here: idealism and pragmatism. Idealistic thinking is the stance that anyone who gives up some of their life-energy for a project deserves to be compensated in a way that helps make their creative pursuit a viable and sustainable source of income. Pragmatic thinking is the understanding that all forms of capitalism are subject to supply and demand and that, like it or not, we have to compete with our peers by either delivering more and/or demanding less.

It's worth noting that these don't have to be seen as mutually exclusive views. It's perfectly fine to agree strongly with both of them. This does, however, leave most people in a conundrum where they feel they are either missing opportunities by demanding to be paid too much, or being ripped off because they are working for too little.

The truth is that there's no universal right answer for every person and every situation. This is the nature of speculation at its heart. When you choose to write a spec script, you choose to speculate a significant amount of life-energy in the hope it pays off by selling in the future – the clue this is speculative is literally in the term *"spec"*. It is, like most forms of business, a calculated gamble. Pretty much every screenwriter trying to break in is speculating so, to a large extent, the debates over working for free are moot – everyone's already busy working for free, often for many years.

When it comes to working for someone else, however, terms have to be agreed and an analysis made if the results are going to be worth the effort. That's hard – incredibly hard – when you don't understand the business or have any experience to go on. Is a one-dollar option on your most prized spec script the best deal you're ever going to get, or will it result in it being locked in a long-term contract when two other entities who want to bid over six figures to acquire it as soon as possible? Is a writing credit for a tiny indie film going to launch your career or create months of painstaking work on a project that's executed terribly and makes your writing look bad? The fact is, nobody really knows. A big part of surviving a long time in the filmmaking world is maintaining a peaceful indifference to what could and couldn't happen.

What we can all do is critically evaluate two factors: what we are giving up from our pie, and what the other party is giving us from theirs. Sacrificing a month of shift work, when we need to pay our rent, so we can write a script on assignment is rather different to giving up a month of evenings that we were going to spend aimlessly watching TV anyway. Spending the last $50 we have to fill up our car so we can be on a set is a very different situation to giving up the $50 we were only ever going to throw away on takeaway pizza.

On the flipside, there's only so much a production can expend, and most aren't swimming in money (like some folks think). The lead producer of a small indie production handing over 3% of the project's budget – as the script fee – may seem meagre when compared to the union rates that studios pay for multi-million dollar movies, but may actually be a very generous offer, given the budget. Maybe the offer also comes with a degree of mentorship, a sole writing credit, and an open invite to be a guest on set.

This unearths an uncomfortable truth; our opportunities are tied to our lifestyles and the affluence of those around us. There is a degree of privilege we may have to accept, and a level of entitlement we may have to compromise on. Something I believe in strongly is the concept of lean-living, where we limit our luxuries as much as possible to maximise our chances of long-term survival within the creative arts. While inequality may be at an all-time high, this has been the stereotypical artist's life for centuries – artists get by on as little as possible because the pursuit of the art means more is pretty much a rite of passage.

Without trying to sound like a "boomer", nobody owes you a new car and a four-bed family home, and I mean no disrespect at all to those who are generally battling their way out of the poverty they were born into; that's an entirely different situation. I say this because I see so many people – usually people who are middle-aged or older – who've had good careers and lived a middle-class lifestyle, become furious when they discover they can't easily sell a screenplay they've spent a few months on, and pay off their mortgage or put their kids through college. Yes, the WGA does stipulate a minimum fee for the creation or purchase of a screenplay, and that fee is a very healthy amount for projects over a certain budget, but these projects represent a minority of the industry overall. The majority have a choice; they make smaller projects that pay people less, or they don't make any projects and thus don't pay anybody at all!

What's important is to feel comfortable with your own decisions and try not to fester any resentment towards the cards you've been dealt. Should you work for free in exchange for experience and exposure? Well, that's pretty much how the entire short film scene fundamentally operates, as directors and most of their cast and crew literally pay to work in the hope their talent gets noticed.

Should you accept 10% of profits on a micro-budget feature and give up your material for free on the basis that the completed movie will be a sure-fire hit? Probably not. Some offers are paradoxically flawed. Sure-fire hits solicit the funding needed to acquire the screenplay they are based on, and smart producers who see that kind of potential would be crazy to give up significant amounts of profit participation (worth millions) over finding the money to pay a $50K script purchase fee.

What is likely is that you're going to be saying *"not now"* (never say *"no"* outright) to a lot of garbage offers in the early years, and the profile of those passes on your part will rise with time until something that feels reasonable to you eventually comes along. As you garner success, you're also going to get a lot of stick from people who will assume you've had it easy. Sadly, many will be unable to see the risks you've taken or the sacrifices you've made because they don't want to accept that's often part of the journey and make those sacrifices themselves.

Hollywood Marches On

Regardless of our own talents and efforts, we have to accept that the Hollywood machine is relentless. Even if we transpire to be the greatest screenwriter in a generation, our presence is not required to maintain the ongoing churn of content needed to drive profit. Not to put too fine a point on it, the industry doesn't care if we're in it or not. Threats to quit, even if we're a known name, mean nothing in the big scheme of things, as does believing we are somehow essential and highly influential.

It's easy to feel rejected by the film business, but it's next to impossible to reject the film business itself.

Breaking into the industry is one thing and surviving for any significant length of time is another. This means it's essential to act professionally, show a backbone, and remain humble. Being difficult to work with *will drive away* collaborators. Being a pushover will see us quickly taken advantage of. Alienating the people we meet on our way up – because we think we don't need them moving forward – will quickly come back to haunt us on the way down. Kind, loyal, confident artists are always going to fare best in a world where so many are cruel, selfish, and secretly plagued by self-doubt.

The path you cut is up to you, but there's lots to be said for starting in the short film world where you can get to grips with refining your process and collaborating with filmmakers. You may not see anything made, you may hate what little is made, and you may see little to no reaction to the things that are made, but you will almost certainly learn a great deal that will serve you well as you take your next step into something like low budget, independent film.

Something you should know, and which may ease some anxiety you have, is that – despite what some say – you don't need to be located in Hollywood itself to build a screenwriting career. I've built mine while being located in Staffordshire within the UK, an area over 5,000 miles away from Los Angeles and a complete contrast to it.

The last three films I've seen made from my scripts were shot within LA. I talk daily with my producing partners who live in LA. I do not feel any pressing need to pack my bags and move to LA. It's important not to be pulled into the fantasy that you're going to land at LAX, and find out your taxi driver knows a producer and can get you a meeting that afternoon to talk about your material. It's far more likely that taxi driver is also an aspiring screenwriter and desperately wants *you* to read their script as soon as possible!

Surviving Production

If you are fortunate enough to get assignments or sell any spec scripts, you'll be entering a new world of pre-production, shooting, post-production, and release that feels daunting. Remind yourself that filmmakers are generally kind people and know that you have been brought in because you're seen as an expert in storytelling.

It's your role to make sure the story itself makes it through to the end with as much integrity and entertainment preserved as possible. It's also important to know that, as the writer, that's where your role also ends.

You need to be a keen and agreeable collaborator, eager to see what others bring to the project.

The best way to look at it is like this: the draft we hand in is our best shot at the movie. That's what we own artistically, and that's what we get to stand beside as a representation of our creative take. The resulting film is owned by everyone involved who's played some role in making it what it is. Be open to things changing from what you've become fixated on in your mind's eye, but also be ready to jump in and say something if the story is being significantly impacted by the decisions of others.

The two most common issues I see cropping up tend to fall into two categories. I call them *Taking the jam out of the doughnut* and *Becoming too self-aware*. The former is a case of cutting or changing something so powerful within the script (usually because of budgets or logistics) it will negatively impact the overall appeal of the finished film significantly. The latter is a case of being so close to the production that inside references (that only mean something to the filmmakers) creep into the final cut. The most extreme case of potentially taking the jam out of the doughnut I've ever faced was during the development and budgeting of one of my spec scripts with a co-producer. This was a *carsploitation*-style script, retrospective in feeling, akin to the B-movies of the seventies and indies of the nineties. Think *True Romance* meets *Thelma & Louise* meets *Vanishing Point*; big car chases, strong women, exciting shootouts, and cool monologues. Edgy, gritty, pulpy.

First, we realised we couldn't afford to do a lot of the stunts because of the budget. Then we realised we couldn't have our big final shootout because logistics meant we couldn't secure the right gas station as a location. Then we were advised strongly by a sales agent to remove the drugs, profanity, and sex because it would limit who we could sell the movie to. That's when we pulled the plug. We quickly realised we now had a doughnut which was quickly becoming all dough and no filling. Yuk! That's when we shifted gears, put that script back in a drawer, and got excited about creating something new and much better aligned to our current situation.

This is the nature of independent film. Everyone can have the best intentions, but various needs cannot be met. The best way I can describe it is to imagine you're trying to produce the script for *Heat* (1995), but you find out you can't afford to shoot the bank heist, can't fit the diner scene into the shooting schedule, and can't use any curse words. Do you still have the same movie you intended to go out and make? Is it really worth going through the cost and energy of producing it?

A film becoming too self-aware is an issue that I see cropping up all the time. Developing, pitching, producing, and shooting a film is an intense, long-term experience where people are liable to become so close to what they're creating that they lose track of the outside audience. One of the most ridiculous examples of this I witnessed was a low-level producer who was so obsessed with referencing a minor character's line from an episode of *Seinfeld* on-set that they started wasting time trying to look up the actor and find out if they were available right away, just so they could make a random appearance in a scene and use the same phrase.

Thankfully, the producer was shut down fast by the director and refocused on what was more pressing before significant time and effort was wasted on creating what would have been nothing more than a jolting and irrelevant moment that only about three people (including said producer) would have found remotely funny.

Of course, how much influence a writer can have standing up for the story during development and production is subject to how much respect they've earned, and how much authority they've been granted. A wise director keeps their writer close but also on a tight-leash; there to lend an ear and opinion, when needed, without running amok and causing confusion. A wise writer also appreciates it's the director's show, and they are there to support – not hinder – at all times, especially when butchering the script is the last resort and the only way forward.

Writers who want to have more control need to consider migrating into directing and/or producing to be in a position where they are a key decision-maker. But they also have to appreciate the responsibility that comes with it. Writers rarely take much flak when a movie is maligned by critics and don't have to face investors should a project bomb commercially. So, be careful what you wish for.

Avoiding The Traps

Our journey into screenwriting is, unfortunately, one that must be made while negotiating a multitude of traps that send us in circles or even in the complete opposite direction of our goals. It's all too easy to make a lot of effort going nowhere if you fall into them.

Some of those traps are laid by ourselves because we fail to see how our own weaknesses drive us to make irrational and self-defeating decisions. The most common need in the early days is the validation that we have what it takes to break in. Tied to this need is typically an impatience for that *big break* moment to come about – where the phone rings or an inbox pings and a whirlwind Hollywood-esque career kicks into life.

Aspiring writers who can find validation from within, and ongoing fulfilment via the act of writing alone, will fair best in the amateur scene. Those who constantly need to hear they have potential and are desperate for a life-changing win will be the most vulnerable. We get to choose which end of the spectrum we fall on by working on mindset, and being realistic about how artistic careers are built.

The reality is that nobody can judge if a writer has what it takes to succeed, and success itself is subject to forces outside of our control. To seek out validation and try to make things happen fast is most likely going to be an exercise in futility that leads to frustration; frustration which can demotivate our efforts, depress our mood, and ironically become self-defeating overall.

Stop Letting Yourself be Coached by the Losers

If you want to survive the dark corners of the filmmaking world by dodging the con artists and ducking the bullshitters, yet the first thing you do is log onto the net and start taking a stranger's opinions on screenwriting as gospel, you have regrettably failed at step one. You're going to have a tough time in pretty much any situation if you are this naive and easily swayed.

Everyone's an expert on what it takes to excel in the film world, it seems, but very few can back up their opinions with personal success stories. This is why doing your due diligence is paramount and something you'll become so used to doing by default that it becomes reflex-like. The better communities out there require users to use their professional names and allow them to easily add their credentials. Nobody hanging out on a forum 12 hours a day while using a fake name and profile pic – who is asking you to *"just trust them"* – is doing so because they are proud of who they are and what they've achieved.

This is the trap, because the people who have the most time and strongest opinions tend to be those who are continually failing, and you're in danger of picking up their bad-think if you don't see through it. Some are a charade, some are deluded and, even if they have the best intentions, they are not talking from direct experience.

The achievers are out there are upfront about who they are and their successes to date. They aren't typically lurking on forums, but they are writing blogs, doing interviews, running podcasts, posting on social media, taking part in panels, and much more, a lot of which is free to consume.

To Many, Your Hope Is
More Valuable Than Gold

It's the mid-1800s, hot but with a refreshing coastal breeze that blusters through a modest settlement called San Francisco. California has caught the gold rush bug that's seeing more and more migrants depart from ships with dollar signs in their eyes and a skip in their steps. There's not much in their pockets, but that doesn't matter because every single one of them believes they will be that rare case that strikes it rich soon, be it through luck or hard labour.

Suddenly, a man paces through the streets with astonishment painted on his face, pausing occasionally to draw a crowd who then flock urgently to their homes or to gather others. In his hand, the man clutches something of wonderment, that when held aloft glistens in the midday sun. "Gold!" he proclaims. "Gold on the American River!" His news triggers a fever that sees every able-bodied person clambering for picks, shovels, and pans, and heading into the hills.

And one really has to ask, why would someone be so stupid as to announce this finding to the world, knowing full well the mania it would spark? Well, you see, this man, this man by the name of Samuel Brannan, has a secret: he owns the only mining goods store between San Francisco and the goldfields, and he recently bought up every pick, shovel, and pan he can find.

Brannan would go on to sell that equipment for 650% profit to the naive but ambitious workforce that had poured from boats and crossed the deserts with nothing to their names. He subsequently became the first millionaire from the California gold rush without ever getting his feet wet or his hands dirty. He was, at best, a capitalist and at worst a con artist; either way, there's a lesson to be learned... hope sells.

In some ways, trying to break into Hollywood, which the vast majority of screenwriters seem to be trying to do, makes panning for gold seem like a sound financial strategy. It's rumoured there are something like 5,000-10,0000 spec scripts written by amateurs each year, equating to an annual wave of a few thousand eager individuals all convinced their obvious talent will be recognised, welcomed, and rewarded. And the thing is, relatively few are buying. The statistics are terrifying, and they get even worse when you consider how Hollywood dominates the industry in the Western World.

The real money for many within the industry is within those churning hordes of writers, many of whom are in the early years and naïve, or stalwarts who've become desperate. This is the true Wild West. Hope is the currency that drives the Hollywood break in economy.

I've said it before, and I'll say it again, but for all the good most services actually do for screenwriters, we may as well set fire to a large pile of money and hope the right producer spots the smoke plume.

Vegas... but Without the Regulation

The best services are ostensibly middlemen, and the worst are parasitic, but it gets worse because every single service out there gets a caveat to put in their Ts&Cs: subjectivity.

You can't objectively evaluate, review, or score something where the majority of its value is subjective. But many try, and then remind you just how asinine it is to have tried – after you've handed over your money, that is. The screenwriting competitions are often lotteries, and the evaluation services often casinos. They boast about their success stories while over 99% of customers walk away with nothing but a bad taste in their mouths. There's no refunds for gamblers.

And we all ask – over and over again – if a script guru knows how to fix amateur scripts... why can't they sell their own scripts? If a pitch specialist can sell a concept... why aren't they a producer? If a reader can see commercial value... why aren't they an executive?

That's not to say that every service out there is in it for the wrong reasons, fundamentally flawed, or a scam. Many believe in what they are doing, some strive to deliver results that help their customers, and a tiny few seem to work. It's just that most are a way to extract easy money from naive and despairing artists, run by people who've failed to break in themselves.

The traps are everywhere, and anyone trying to reach for your wallet needs to be treated with a high degree of scepticism. Yes, there's good information locked away in some of those books, and there are opportunities via some of those services, but any writer would be wise to look at the success stories first – not testimonials, not press releases, not anecdotal forum messages – like, actually Google the writers listed and find out where they are now and hope they weren't that dude who was asking you to read their script last week.

> There are so many people out there charging you money to enter contests, charging you money for notes, charging you money for consulting. It doesn't work. And more to the point, not doing it has worked. In fact, not doing it has worked for literally everyone you and I know who works as a professional screenwriter. So, at some point, I think we're asking people to take a leap of faith here and stop doing this. We know that the Nicholls Fellowship matters. It doesn't always work, but it can work. We know that Austin, to a lesser extent, can work. Beyond that, stop.

Craig Mazin, Scriptnotes, Ep 355

You have to stop staring directly into the glitzy bright light because it can be blinding. You have to turn your back on the self-appointed doormen who want to shake you down for what little change you have. Ultimately though, you have to slow down and realise there's more to all this than chasing some elusive gold nuggets in the bottom of a river.

You have been warned. Your mindset will have a huge impact on your vulnerability, and there's plenty of people out there ready to exploit any desperation you allow to fester. There's story after story – going back over a century – of screenwriters simply patiently honing their craft while networking in a professional manner until they align with the right people, sometimes in the strangest but most serendipitous ways, until they eventually start seeing success. Simply follow the well-trodden path and stay on it when it gets a little rocky.

My Mistakes with Career Building

As I write this, I'm approaching ten years since I wrote my first screenplay back in 2012. It wasn't until 2018 that I got my first commissioned assignment and thus, with some highly impressive finger math, I can adjudicate that 60% of my time spent screenwriting has been trying to break in and turn my passion into a sustainable career. I often tell people to give it at least ten years to see significant traction in screenwriting and therefore consider myself one of the lucky ones. I did, however, waste quite a few years getting it all wrong.

Like many first-time fiction writers, I completed a story I was very proud of but had no idea what to do with next. On the one side, the typical route to success seemed simple: secure a screenwriting agent and start seeing sales and assignments. However, it also seemed ungraspable due to the insulated world most reps hide within and the fact I knew nobody in the industry. This new world seemed scary, and only for those with bold personalities and a refusal to take a "no", so like most first time writers, I made the mistake of shying away from it and went back to my safe place – writing in isolation.

I actually buried myself in novel writing because my hobby was now a form of therapy and at least novel writers got to self-publish their work and get a shot at the brass ring that is the consumer market. I spent every waking moment first converting my existing screenplay into a novella and then writing another complete novel. I was a typing machine, avoiding the foreboding world of networking and self-promotion (that I should have been tackling under the guise that more material needed to come first).

I was, however, also listening to the Podcast series *Scriptnotes* by John August and Craig Mazin that turned me on to a new website service that seemed to have the answer for aspiring unknown screenwriters who needed to get their scripts read. This website allowed people to buy evaluations and get their material scored and ranked – the higher the score, the more exposure they would get. I was sold on the concept. This was the answer to the supply and demand problem Hollywood was facing. I was convinced that scripts could be scored objectively and was about to get a *harsh* lesson in subjectivity!

I'll save the emotional side for the next chapter on Happiness & Creativity but, needless to say, the results did nothing for my career prospects or my motivation because, for every reader that loved my material and boosted it up, there was another that hated it and knocked it back down. I was quickly back to square one with my wallet significantly lighter. I concluded, foolishly, that I was simply using the wrong type of service and turned to these screenwriting competitions I'd heard of instead. People had told me that a high placement in a competition was a guaranteed golden key into Hollywood. All I had to do was become a finalist or win one, and there were quite a few to enter, so I may as well start preparing my Oscar acceptance speech now. Therefore, I entered a few of those too, waited a few months while I wrote new material, and didn't get any further than the quarter-finals. Damn. The 'plan' was to get lucky and have my genius acknowledged.

I was now aware of querying (where a screenwriter sends a premise to industry members and asks if they'd like to read the script) but had no contacts, so I turned to buying mailing lists supposedly packed with interested parties. After sending out a stream of emails to various info@ addresses, I got a stream of 'recipient not found' replies in return, as most bounced back undelivered. I got three read requests that went nowhere. I even paid to pitch, so to speak, in the form of buying opportunities to query what were apparently a few hungry producers who, it turned out, didn't have an appetite for what I was serving up.

This all felt exhausting, especially on top of writing as much as I could in my spare time, and *it was exhausting*. It was exhausting because I was pushing too hard and doing things in the hardest and most unrewarding way possible. It was expensive too, and eating away at what little savings I had, making my life feel increasingly perilous. Worse still, I was desperate for validation. Nobody had confirmed I had what it took, and I was starting to fear I didn't have it.

A remarkable thing did happen during all of this, however. One of my scripts was picked out and highlighted, out of thousands of others, on the Amazon Studios website back when they were taking amateur submissions. But, despite being on the front page of their site, in the Notable Projects section, the phone didn't start ringing off the hook and I took the silence as confirmation I didn't have anything worth offering.

By this point, I was a regular in the DoneDealPro forum community, where it seemed like everyone else was part of the higher echelons of the industry. So many had these strong viewpoints on how everything worked and what it took to succeed. One particularly frequent contributor, who'd had more success on the evaluation and scoring website I'd initial tried, and who had managed to query their way to securing a manager, wrote a damning diatribe on how so many amateurs were wasting their time if they couldn't achieve a certain evaluation score or get to a certain round in the competitions. Amateurs just like me. Their argument was brash but convincing; convincing enough that what little motivation I had drained from my body and I couldn't keep pushing anymore. I was only two years into chasing my dream, and my weariness finally faded into burnout.

I crashed.

I felt like a deluded hack and had the low scores, competition failures, lack of read-requests, along with the harsh advice of another writer, to prove it.

I actually tried to give up, which was probably even more naive than trying to break into Hollywood, given that writing was my happy place. I switched to the – much friendlier at the time – Stage 32 Screenwriting Lounge community, which was more supportive, and shared what I had learned there. The guy behind the site, Richard "RB" Botto, really empathised with my plight and admired my viewpoints, giving me a platform to blog about my experiences and build my self-confidence. Before long, I started to become part of a group of people I saw as peers rather than bullies, with the added benefit they were using real names and occasionally shared real credits. Giving up hadn't been the mistake; it had been the first sensible thing I'd done in a long time because it made me realise giving up was never an option. It forced me to take the breather I needed to find a more mutually supportive community.

My writing, however, was suffering more than ever as I continued to try to figure out what this crazy industry wanted and come up with a Goldilocks script nobody could refuse. I didn't see how ridiculous that was and took on a lot of bad advice and fear from people I wasn't doing my due diligence on. I was probably a better writer in some aspects of the craft, such as writing shorter scenes within a better story structure, but I had no direction or voice. I had gone from writing pulpy, hard-hitting thrillers to young adult fantasies in a bid to jump on a trend.

Lost and desperate once again, I returned to that evaluation site like a drunk falling off the wagon and handed over the last of my savings as a Hail Mary. The numbers came in, and they were worse than ever. As if that wasn't damning enough, a writer turned consultant who'd been killing it in the competition scene messaged to inform me that, even after reading just one page of my most highly-acclaimed script, they'd concluded I seriously needed the help of a *"professional writer"* such as her.

This was my lowest point because, on top of feeling like I simply didn't have the talent, nothing seemed to make any sense anymore and the few opportunities that seemed to exist felt locked off behind paywalls. I concluded I didn't have the ability, the connections, or the money to even begin to chip away at my dream, but I also knew I couldn't stop writing either.

There was this tiny glimmer of light still there. Within those first two years of writing, I had optioned a short script to an aspiring young director by the name of Sandra Mitrovic, who was studying film in London at the time. Thanks to her remarkable production experience throughout her childhood and teenage years, she did a brilliant job turning the words into reality. I'd made the mistake of not taking the short film scene seriously enough. After all, the short film made from my script had been screened at the film school, and that was it. Nothing seemingly came of it. But a film had been made from my words nonetheless. What I gradually came to realise – in that pit of despair – was that this WAS my validation, and it WAS a viable path forward. Filmmakers at this level wanted to produce my material and, even if they failed to do so, their eagerness and effort had to be appreciated. Was it all I had? Yes. But it was something I could lean into and use to see some positive, motivating results while writing the kind of pulpy content I loved.

So, I did something that seemed a little crazy. I stopped writing feature scripts altogether, and I started writing short scripts instead. I also walked away from some toxic screenwriting communities and turned my attention to books on screenwriting, fiction-writing in general, artistry, and filmmaking history. I consumed information either written by, or written about, successful people while writing one or two short scripts a week and offering those to filmmakers for free. This coincided perfectly with the increasing popularity of the *Shootin' The Shorts* project run by Janet Goodman-Clarke, which was highlighting short scripts to filmmakers visiting the brilliant SimplyScripts website. Janet saw something in my work, and her positive reviews saw me connecting with a multitude of directors and actors who loved what I was writing and wanted to be part of it. The system was working: study the craft > apply it with passion > connect with people who love the results.

Meanwhile, I was also being asked back more and more by Stage 32 to blog about my journey into screenwriting, and this gave me the courage to start blogging independently, something that felt a lot healthier and constructive than sitting on forums all day and, over time, drew in a growing circle of like-minded friends who became my champions.

Despite a few dozen short script options, next to none of those projects ever got made, while some that did missed the mark completely and wasted good material. One or two nailed it but went nowhere in terms of exposure. I never got a big break in the short film world, but I learned so much outside of screenwriting itself from the experience, developed my storytelling craft to a high level, and found my artistic voice as a result. I knew what I wanted to write, how to write it, and that there were people out there who appreciated it. This was a very real marketplace, and I was serving it. I had direct experience of working with producers, directors, and actors from pre-production to shooting to release. I'd had a mini filmmaking boot camp at zero financial cost and, while the results were much like the bigger world of feature films, the mistakes both myself and others may have made had a much smaller impact overall.

As my confidence and profile rose, the profile of people reaching out to me rose with it. Many of them were filmmakers who didn't quite have what it took to helm a feature, some were deluded, and a few were outright hucksters trying to scam me. It was my experience in the short film world and reading into the lives of successful screenwriters that allowed me to see that. The nibbles I was getting were all *"jam tomorrow"* type offers where the promised money was never going to come in and a worthy film unlikely to be produced.

So, I kept my head down, stayed away from the evaluation services and competitions, stayed away from the forum trolls and opportunists, and went back to writing feature scripts with my newfound voice and a better grasp of storytelling craft. I continued to blog to an increasingly growing audience of supporters and also started putting together an early version of the Turn & Burn screenwriting guide while building my own platform for exposure in the form of Script Revolution. I continued to read the books and watch the documentaries on filmmaking, too, without looking for one answer that solved everything and instead looked to add more viewpoints to my arsenal. I wrote some of the best material I've ever written, and I wrote it without any fear of what people would think or the feverish urgency it should pay off. I didn't go out and query because people were coming to me now based on recommendations and awareness.

I got my first offer of a feature script option from a credited producer in Vancouver in 2017, incidentally a day before my birthday and on the night I was attending the premiere by a small local filmmaker. That didn't pan out with the funding, but it did immeasurable things for my self-confidence and patience. In early 2018 I was contacted by long-time filmmaker, Emmy award winner, and global box office #1 producer, Shane Stanley, who'd read some of my blogs and wondered if my scripts lived up to my opinions – thankfully, in his eyes, at least, they did. Shane is now one of my best friends, a producing partner, and we're currently making our third feature film together. I got to go to LA, I got to meet some of my heroes, I got to shake hands with some of my champions, and that whole amazing experience is a book in itself.

These days, I get validation on a near-daily basis from respected industry members who admire my work. I wish I could go back and tell that despairing writer I once was that it would come to me eventually because I made the mistake of feeling so much pain I never needed to feel. And no, I still don't have an agent or a manager because I'm not chasing anything or anybody. I'm letting my work speak for itself and relationships grow organically. Rather than wait for permission to get in front of producers, I became a producer.

The biggest mistake I made for years was allowing fear and desperation to push and pull me in directions that were fundamentally self-destructive. It caused me to listen to people who didn't really know what they were talking about and buy into solutions that operated more like casinos and lotteries than fair exposure platforms. The answer was in the most humble places rather than the most glamourous. The solution was to work slowly up from the bottom rather than wait for a life-changing event to catapult me to the top.

Needless to say, this had a huge impact on my mental health and wellbeing which itself influenced my creativity – both positively and negatively – and *that topic* will form the basis of the next chapter!

CHAPTER 8: HAPPINESS AND CREATIVITY

Perhaps this title should read *"The Ongoing Evasion of Sadness and Mediocrity"*. There's no getting away from the fact that waves of extreme sadness go hand in hand with the life of a creative – hell, some would argue it actually fuels many of us.

The thing is, being continually down is a very unhealthy way to live, regardless of any supposed artistic benefits. Things get extremely dark for many people – it has done for me, and I'd rather be sticking around – because life has a great deal more to offer than the continual headfuck of trying to break into professional screenwriting and maintain a career in the film industry. So, here's some musing on the subject of that elusive but essential part of any screenwriter's life: happiness.

Depression, Anxiety, and Writer Madness

Firstly, I want you to know I've been there and I've been there for an extended period of time. I know what it's like to spiral down into a very dark and lonely place and, after spending years crawling out, still have to fight hard occasionally not to get dragged back into the void. So, this isn't someone writing from the outside looking in.

I'm very open about the mental health issues I've suffered and still struggle with to this day. I talk about it because it needs to be discussed, and it saddens me that the topic isn't discussed more within our communities. Thankfully, that does seem like it's starting to change.

I also appreciate how many writers have been, currently are, and will be sucked into a negative cycle. Creativity is, in a way, a crutch for our daily emotions, and it's all too easy to become obsessed not only with the craft but also validation from peers and success in the form of being widely appreciated. I know what it's like to lie awake at night, thinking about what I want – no NEED – to sit down and write so people will spot my talent and life will fall into place. I know what it's like to forget to eat and not realise I'm losing weight until my jeans start falling down, or how crossing my bony legs feels like trying to settle down on a cattle grid. I know what it's like for my jaw and eyes to ache from sobbing on a daily basis, what it's like to zone out of normal life, to take every bit of negative feedback like a cold knife to the heart, to listen incessantly to the tormenting voice in my head, to plan my own suicide in detail, and not so much set a date to go through with it, but to simply hang around to see when my shell of a body commits to doing it.

If you are living like this, you need to stop here and seek help immediately. No good can come of it. Recovery can come faster than you think. Nobody lost anything by regaining their happiness.

The first step is to reach out to somebody and tell them. If they don't listen, tell somebody else. If you have to, pick yourself up from the ground. Eat well. Exercise regularly. Laugh at the nonsense that voice in your head comes out with because it's not the real you. Look at cognitive behavioural therapy (CBT). Google 'mindfulness' to help you feel present. Everybody can be helped. Stop writing and take a breath if you feel like it; the longer you are going to be around, the more time you have to do the things you really need to do… and have people appreciate you for doing them.

Working yourself to death isn't perseverance. Burning out isn't perseverance. Taking a moment in your life to regain your strength and carry on is perseverance.

The Answer

I'm not going to beat around the bush, tease, or build up to some game-changing conclusion. The fundamental answer to finding happiness in writing is to LOVE THE PROCESS OF WRITING ITSELF. Everything expands outward from the process.

Let's get that over with.

There is no getting away from the process. It will always be there regardless of any struggle or success. There may be other huge issues in your life that are affecting your wellbeing, and may need addressing to fix, but writing itself is all about the process and, if it's something that no longer fills you with joy and fulfilment, something has gone wrong.

You almost certainly loved writing at some point, and that's why you are where you are now. It was probably therapeutic when you started and, while perhaps exhausting and challenging, it was ultimately fun. Many of us lose that fun element as anxiety, paranoia, stress, doubt, and impatience creep into our everyday efforts to chase our dreams. Exhausting and challenging becomes flogging and flailing while the fun gets replaced with productivity.

Many writers, especially those who've been trying to break in for some time, talk about the writing process as a miserable grind that must be struggled through to succeed. These are writers who will make statements such as *"hate writing, love having written"*, and they are unhealthy creatives to listen to because they normalise hating the one element we cannot avoid. We can choose not to chase a career, we can choose not to write in a certain genre, we can choose only to write in a certain medium, but we absolutely cannot choose to ignore the call and evade the act of writing itself.

Misery loves company, so there's plenty of people out there who want to dwell collectively in that negative headspace, reminding others of how resentful they are toward this form of art while recruiting as many others as possible to bitch and moan about their predicament. Sadly, many of these people are opinion leaders in the form of speakers and consultants, and I'm not going to make many friends saying this but, they're miserable because they've failed miserably at becoming the writers they want to be.

Look, hating the writing process because it hasn't turned into the career you want is like hating your car because you resent the journey or hating your garden because of the weather. You're taking something close to you, something that should empower you and offer solace, and unfairly turning it into a monster you'll instinctively want to flee from.

Re-finding our love of the process isn't as hard as it may appear, even with all the evidence and experience we may have gathered to justify our cynicism and pessimism. It's a choice.

It Isn't Romantic, It Isn't Academic... but It Absolutely Is Art

On the flip-side, learning to love the process doesn't mean idolising some sort of naive fantasy where we spring out of bed each morning bursting with great ideas and type merrily away at a computer until midnight. This is a ridiculous goal to aim for, but I fear many (ironically, a lot of miserable writers) see it as a realistic ideal, often believing it's how their heroes go about their day. The act of building an entire universe, populated with well-developed characters engaged in a captivating plot, interwoven with a resounding philosophical message, all so you can hopefully stand out within one of the most competitive professional fields in the world, is a daunting journey to take the first step on, never mind walk in entirety. But this is exactly *why* we should love the process, because it's where the hard work is done and, if you haven't noticed, work doesn't feel quite so hard when you're competent, empowered, motivated, and prepared.

All this means being pragmatic about what we need to do and how we go about doing it while refusing to see it as an academic exercise or professional chore. The appreciation we receive will not be tied to the workload we choose to take on. I see too many aspiring writers boasting about their word count, or page count, or how many drafts they've already written as if waiting for a gold star to materialise out of thin air. School teaches us that success is an objective grade, subject to effort, research, hitting criteria, and presentation. The corporate world also programs us into believing that being servile and diligent is the key to staying employed and getting promotions, all subject to a job interview where we carefully walk the tightrope of trying to appear flawless. Again, we're encouraged to appear busy and chase conformity so as not to upset the wrong person and lose everything. We have to unlearn a lot of this for fear of being driven to insanity.

That typo-ridden screenplay written in a few days that's full of factual errors and contains a few plot holes might just entertain a producer far more than your highly-polished and thoroughly scrutinised epic that took you years of rewrites to turn into an "acceptable" draft. That's how it goes, and it typically goes that way because one writer's love of the process came through stronger in the pages. This isn't to say that being lazy and sloppy is somehow better or a goal to aim for, just that determination is most fruitful when it's driven by an infectious passion.

Art is a fickle and mysterious mistress and, while many people don't want to accept this, screenwriting is an artistic pursuit. In fact, I think many don't want to accept that screenwriting is a form of art because that means accepting the life of an artist that comes with it. That's daunting when you don't really know what it entails. What does it entail? An inherent passion to pursue a playful curiosity and (via that exploration) to create a form of cultural medicine that can be shared with others. That's what it entails.

Note the term *"playful curiosity"* here, and the lack of a monetary reward as the motivation. True artists do what they do because they are rewarded by the act of exploration, discovery, and giving itself, right from the moment a new idea comes into their heads. You've most likely experienced this yourself in the form of daydreaming and sharing those dreams with others, which you wouldn't choose to do unless you really enjoyed doing it.

You may have also dreamt up ideas while talking to another person and gotten more and more excited as you build and build on the fiction you have created together. I bet, in fact, that you've had an absolute blast thinking up ideas and felt incredibly motivated to turn them into prose right up to the point you've sat down in front of a computer and suddenly found the wind has been taken from your sails. This is often the problem, and it's brought on by utilising a process that disheartens rather than encourages.

You're reading this book because I built a process that works for me. I share it in the hope it will work for you and many others. I encourage you to try it and only keep using it if it makes your writing easier and more fun. Yes! Say it with me! EASIER AND MORE FUN! If it doesn't click with you, then please try as many other approaches as you can until you have something that does.

Chase What Really Matters

I've yet to hear of any screenwriter reaching some kind of pinnacle in their career where all their worries and fears drained from them. If you care a great deal about being talented, being appreciated, and being valuable now, you won't stop caring about that later. Watch the documentary *Seduced & Abandoned* (2013) and note how Alec Baldwin struggles to get a movie funded, and how Francis Ford Coppola once became so upset he couldn't get a new project off the ground he threw his Oscars out of a window.

This is the reality many don't want to witness or accept. There is no mountain top in which to place a flag and call it a day. Becoming a finalist in a competition isn't the end; just like getting a read request, selling a spec, getting a script produced, or getting critical acclaim isn't the end. History is littered with creative after creative who've found huge audiences and huge fortunes only to feel the same (if not worse) than they did when they started because they've become distanced from the process, or it's turned ugly for them. Many of those artists simply cannot understand why they feel so bad when, on paper, their life seems so good. We see it in other forms of the creative arts; the musician who gets a record deal but forgets their roots, the actor who sells out and loses respect from their fans, and the same principle absolutely exists within screenwriting too. Our relationship with the process always remains, regardless of our successes, so it's essential we find peace with it and do not let it get caught up with our career aspirations.

Example: In the book *Hollywood Animal,* legendary writer Joe Eszterhas details his journey from senior editor for Rolling Stone magazine to Hollywood screenwriter. A sucker for research, Eszterhas would take his time to not only travel across America to study the subjects of his writing but also integrate into their worlds for an extended time. This methodology got results for him with *F.I.S.T.* (1978) starring Sylvester Stallone, which was a huge hit at the box office.

When back home writing, however, this bullish man who seemed to fear no one or anything was privately dealing with an issue where he'd have to vomit every morning before writing, and he didn't know why. This went on for three years until he received what he describes as the "best writing advice he ever got" from *Sophie's Choice* (1982) producer Alan J. Pakula. After Eszterhas turned in a very poor draft of his latest script, Pakula told him to forget the research, stop looking for real-life people to base his characters on, and instead make everything up. Eszterhas did just that, had the most fun he'd ever had writing a screenplay, and immediately stopped throwing up in the mornings. What he'd been suffering from before was stress. Stress brought on by unreasonable pressure he'd put on himself to write something accurate over something artistic. His existing writing process hadn't been healthy for him at all, while his new one let his inner artist shine. Joe Eszterhas would famously go on to sell his *Basic Instinct* script for $3m after a bidding war, and secure a front fee of $2m to write *Showgirls* based on the idea he quickly scribbled onto a napkin. These two movies alone would go on to earn a billion dollars.

Careers aren't just built on talent, though; they're built on luck and personality too, which can sometimes make them a poor barometer of artistry. Some artists can make the mistake of attributing a lack of success as being down to a lack of talent, while other artists can feel imposters despite success. Both issues are rooted in them allowing the writing process to go from something they love to something they loathe.

In some ways, all the stress and anxiety we can feel when writing is the curse of having a vibrant imagination that paints an intense image of what lies ahead for us. We have to remind ourselves that, while we have the ability to picture success vividly, it's unreasonable to expect reality to meet our expectations, even if we hold up our end of the deal. We have to learn to enjoy writing now and quit stressing about the future. This isn't just so we can tackle working in film; there's a huge break in industry standing between us and the production world that targets new writers from day one. Some of it's good, a lot of it's bad, and it trades off the constant churn of amateur writers trying to monetise their hobby.

If you have a script you want to sell, there's a crowd of hungry hucksters fighting to dig into your pockets while planting enough self-doubt in your mind to make sure you keep coming back for guidance, reassurance, and what looks like opportunity. It's a marketplace that regularly impoverishes and destroys screenwriters who fall foul of its tactics and lose track of what matters.

We have to remind ourselves of our values regularly; why did we get into writing in the first place? Was it to de-stress? Did it start as a career aspiration, or did it gradually morph into one? The second that trying to sell a script (or get an assignment) takes over our wellbeing, we have to stop and take a step back because it can stir up a mania that abuses our work and hampers our progress.

Let Finding Self-Love Be Your Success Story

Loving the process of writing stems from loving yourself as a writer. That can be impossible to do if we see ourselves as inadequate or even hate the things that make us unique. We have to assure ourselves that, as of today and despite all our failings and weaknesses, we are enough, and what may make us weird also makes us special. There is no good reason to live in self-subjected pain, as the misery that comes with it can creep into our work and cause a vicious downward spiral.

I've seen too many writers chasing validation in its various forms (evaluation scores, competition placements, coverage ratings, etc.), taking what mixed feedback they have, and butchering their work in the hope it fixes all the "problems" in their script. They then run it through the same system again only to have it perform worse and repeat the process over and over, continually going downward and getting more lost and frustrated along the way while eventually concluding the core problem must be themselves in the form of their lack of talent and their unlikeable subject matter.

Instead, we want the complete reversal, an upward spiral where we begin with rewriting our own internal dialogue. *"I don't know enough about the craft"* becomes *"I'm always learning more about the craft"*. *"I only write dumb action movies"* becomes *"I love writing exciting movies that anyone can enjoy"*. *"I've achieved nothing of significance"* becomes *"I'm still in the game and setting new goals"*.

Some would say this is sappy, toxic positivity, and it certainly is if it's fuelled by nothing but delusion rather than pragmatism. It's essential we maintain a realistic balance by appreciating the very real things we've achieved, are achieving, and which we can go on to achieve. This is, to a degree, choosing to stop and smell the roses; those roses being us and our art. We can appreciate ourselves objectively and love ourselves unconditionally.

Simply logging our achievements is a powerful way to create an upward spiral. Just the date and a short entry in a text document will do. Those early wins might be writing our first treatment or finishing our first script before migrating to getting that first read or connecting with that important contact, before it becomes getting that green light or attaching that actor, until eventually it becomes releasing that movie or receiving that big award. These things build over time, and it's important to be able to look back at any point and see that process of growth and causality taking place year after year.

The same goes for compliments. Negative comments tend to burn themselves into our minds so they'll be remembered forever while compliments run off us like water off a duck's back. It pays to note them down and revisit them, because seeing ourselves through the eyes of others can be a powerful way to build pride in who we really are.

All this isn't any more weak and needy than a top athlete logging their stats, displaying their awards, and meeting their fans. It's healthy to nurture our wellbeing and unhealthy to neglect it. Life's hard enough without our creative passion tormenting us in addition. There's no prize for most exhausted, most undervalued, or most dejected screenwriter, even if we do live in a world where working ourselves to an early death is seen as a badge of honour.

As freelancers, we must be both a good boss and a good worker rather than becoming both the manager and the employee from hell in our own lives. We have to set realistic deadlines, establish achievable goals, support our learning, and invest in our opportunities while also maintaining a schedule, rising to the occasion, tackling our weaknesses, and making the most of what's on offer. Ultimately, we have to be accountable for not only our progress but also our happiness.

Value Your Voice

If you're struggling with what the term 'artistic voice' means, try to think of it as an aesthetic. It's a combination of a multitude of different elements about you that create an eclectic cocktail. People want to spend time with you, be around you, and enjoy your energy because your aesthetic creates a vibe with them that feels rewarding to experience.

Think about a location you love. That place will have its own unique aesthetic. I love New York City. I love the neo-gothic architecture, the street pizza, and the Con Edison steam network. I love how it's so busy you blend into the background, the chorus of honking horns, and the way people are brash on the surface yet saints underneath. I love the whole NYC attitude, the landmarks, and even the rats that populate the subway. I love a very long list of other things, too, some of which I'm not even fully aware of that help make up that landscape, and while many other places have the same elements, they don't have them in the same blend and extremities as The Big Apple. That's what makes it special. That's its voice.

Your voice will be hardest to see from within, and it may take both some winding back to take in the bigger picture, and some zooming in to analyse the detail. A good place to find it is in your earliest work when you didn't have the fear and reservations you have now. What you probably do notice right now, however, is your 'weird'; the quirks about your attitude and writing which stick out as oddball. You might see it as a problem, a perennial issue that's causing an obstacle that holds you back. This is a huge mistake many of us make, especially if someone does pick up on it negatively. The reality is your weird is probably only holding you back if you're not leaning into it enough. If you find everything you write turns into a zany comedy, and that's compromising the serious thriller you're trying to write, you're failing to see the wood for the trees. Your weird isn't compromising the ordinary; the ordinary is compromising your weird! The real problem is you're trying to write a serious thriller when your soul wants to indulge in something it finds wackier and funnier.

EMBRACE THY WIERD, just like your heroes have. Van Gogh, Dr. Seuss, David Lynch, Bowie, Steven King, Banksy, Charlie Kaufman, Lady Gaga, and Wes Anderson are all weird and have created remarkable content that's connected with huge audiences. People generally pride themselves on their crazy, so why wouldn't you – as an artist who wants to stand out – do precisely that, rather than trying to blend in? This doesn't mean you have to be wacky or zany; weird comes in many, many forms. It just means you have to be authentic, accept who you really are, and give yourself permission to share what you truly love doing with the world. They say, *"write the movies you want to watch"*, so it's time to ask yourself if you're truly doing that or if you're actually trying to write the movies you think studio execs want to make.

Example: In 2012, the hip-hop duo Macklemore & Ryan Lewis had a sleeper hit with their track *Thrift Shop*, a pop-rap song about buying second-hand goods as cheaply as possible that ran contrary to the ostentatious "bling" culture at the time. Featuring a catchy saxophone hook and comical lyrics, the track went to number one in nine countries, sold 6 million copies in the US alone, and has since received 1.5 billion views for its music video on YouTube.

For Macklemore and Lewis, there was one catch, *Thrift Shop* was not representative of their typical musical style. It was an outlier made in a moment of inspiration. With their newfound international popularity and demand for them to tour, they knew those who had fallen in love with their big hit (and wanted more of that kind of thing) might have felt alienated when they heard their usual repertoire instead. Macklemore and Lewis stuck to their artistic voice, continued to make and perform the kind of music they were rooted in, and put their faith in their audience supporting their direction. Much of that audience did indeed come with them; the duo have a second Hot 100 Chart number one to their name, have recorded two highly successful albums, and also won numerous high-profile awards.

Recognising and embracing our voice as early as possible is not only important because it can help us break in, but because – should we see success – we need to remain grounded by the fundamentals that drive and fulfil us. Through fear, we become lost or, worse still, sell-out and gradually become a parody of what we're best known for.

Reset, Refresh, & Revisit

It might be that you're feeling lost, and that's common for writers who have been trying to break in for some time as they have consumed and suppressed so much information, a lot of which is conflicting, and that's pulling them in different directions. This is a good time to hit the pause button.

Firstly, we have to ask ourselves a very difficult question during this juncture; is screenwriting really our dream? If there's any moment of doubt, we must investigate that and re-evaluate our life goals. Is this still our true passion? Are we really prepared to potentially lose everything and go through hell to be one of the 0.0001% who break in? If not, then it's maybe time to make changes that may be as drastic as pulling the rip-cord and ejecting from the world of screenwriting entirely to find a more desirable career path. If we're still driven to continue, then there's certainly no harm in confirming that quitting isn't an option.

Now's a good time to put our feet up and effectively rehabilitate ourselves from the lost, anxious, and paranoid artist we've become. Books are a good place to start. I recommend reading *Writing for Emotional Impact* by Karl Iglesias, *Art & Fear* by David Bayles & Ted Orland, and *Tales from the Script* by Peter Hanson and Paul Robert

Herman, along with a list of other books detailed in the Further Reading chapter. The three I've highlighted, however, are the most powerful books I've read that cover screenwriting craft, finding fulfilment through art, and the nature of a career in the film business. These are the three pillars of knowledge we can always be building; how to write better stories, how to produce meaningful art, and how to pay the bills.

It's powerful to rewatch our favourite films and remind ourselves of those artistic voices that have impacted us over our lives. We can watch them in a way that does them justice too on the biggest screen possible, and with the best sound, that gets us as close as possible to the original movie theatre experience. Many of these will likely be cult classics where material exists on how they were made along with analysis of the story and filmmaking tricks. You might be very surprised with what you learn as we tend to picture the movies we love as having been made brilliantly under perfect conditions and with unwavering confidence.

Example: As mentioned in a previous chapter, the *Mad Max* movies were one of the biggest film influences in my life and, until I studied how the films were made, I assumed George Miller and Byron Kennedy decided to make an apocalyptic car chase movie one day, and that was pretty much that – an iconic film was made and went on to become one of the most profitable in history.

I didn't realise that the genesis of a "road cop" movie went as far back as Kennedy's silent filmmaking over a decade before, and the initial script – which took three years to write – pulled very heavily from *Stone* (1974) a biker revenge movie featuring a cop that they even used five actors from. They also pulled from *Dirty Mary, Crazy Larry* (1974) which has lines paraphrased from it (along with the concept of a custom-built "police interceptor"), *Lawrence of Arabia* (1962) which visually inspires many of the scenes, and the *Heavy Metal* comic books that Miller wanted to use the title from and eventually imitated the logo of. I didn't know that Miller & Kennedy couldn't understand why the film was so successful and hadn't even heard of *The Hero's Journey* until they travelled to Hollywood. Likewise, I didn't know *Mad Max 2* appears to borrow very heavily from *The Ultimate Warrior* (1975) which has the same plot, *Ben-Hur* (1959) with the chariot racing, *Lawrence of Arabia*, again, with the final crash, *Shane* (1953) with the feral kid, and *A Boy and His Dog* (1975) with the dog as a companion to the anti-hero. It goes on and on. I only came to know this thanks to the hard work of people like the Mad Max Bible channel on YouTube and it blew my mind how much had already been done in the film world before Miller & Kennedy did it in their own special way. Once again, my heroes turned out to be normal human beings working under ordinary conditions, inspired by the content they consumed and fusing much of that together with their own original ideas under a unique artistic voice.

In addition to your favourite films' production histories, it's also worth looking at the reaction from audiences over time. Were the movies universally admired from day one? Were they polarising in their critical reviews or even hated? What was the box office performance like, compared to that of home video and DVD? Did they initially go by unnoticed, only to find cult status in time?

On top of all this, there's something else we need to be looking for… the patterns that connect all our cherished films together in terms such as genre, tone, premise, characters, action, location, and theme. We can take our own work and aspirations and see where it fits among all this. There should be a clear link that again helps us solidify our voice and reassure us there's a keen audience out there waiting for our material.

The final question we have to ask ourselves, and this can be a tough pill to swallow, is how well would our favourite films from our past realistically perform if they were released in today's marketplace? Would they even make it into the movie theatre? Would they connect and resound in today's culture? Would they compete with the kind of films that are currently on the big screen? This is important because, while there's certainly nothing wrong with writing something that feels relatively small and retrospective, expecting it to perform at the box office like the films it harks back to might be ridiculous. It seems like so many older writers have yet another campy space opera they want to see turned into a franchise and expect a big studio to throw a nine-figure sum at, while forgetting it's no longer 1973.

Enjoy the Journey at a Steady Pace

I am, at the time of writing, probably about five to ten years from making the films I *really* want to make; in other words, the films I want to be known for artistically. The films that are pure and unadulterated CJ Walley. I love the films I am making now. I'm proud of them and feel blessed to be making them. They are very close to where my artistic voice thrives, but there are obstacles on my own journey I have yet to overcome before I can turn my spec scripts into the films I see in my head. I'm cool with that, and I'm more than happy to continue in the direction I'm headed. Being comfortable with being patient pays dividends.

You can have a plan, or you can have an attitude, and it's the latter that serves the art world best. As screenwriters, we absolutely cannot realistically make things happen or predict what's going to happen. Even the big studios struggle to do this and, despite huge investments into marketing and consumer research, typically suffer something like an 80% fail rate with their projects. We cannot predict if our voice is going to appeal, which industry members we're going to connect with, what gets green-lit should we work together, if a production is going to go smoothly, or if the finished film is going to be well received. There are so many variables before we even get onto the topic of subjectivity, and it's fair to say we can't even guarantee we'll finish the next spec we set out to write. Forming a plan such as writing a certain number of screenplays in a certain amount of time, advancing to a certain level in a competition next year, or selling a spec before a certain age is madness that's only likely to trigger disappointment and frustration later down the line; that failure only exists because we decided to set those goals in the first place.

What we can do, instead, is move forward with a clear and considered attitude. Please note that this isn't the same as having no plan at all and simply seeing what happens. An attitude might be to focus entirely on writing within one genre and reaching out proactively to independent producers who specialise in that genre. It might be to blog openly and authentically about our struggles while slowing down our pace and taking more time to develop our stories. It can be a limitless combination of many, many things, but it has to be an attitude that's healthy for us right now, and it has to be organic and adaptable as our situation and knowledge change. When people ask us, *"So, what's your plan?"* our answer can be something like, *"Well, I'm going to double-down on writing single-location thrillers that can be made on shoestring budgets while putting myself out there in the social media circles that low-budget filmmakers hang out in"* rather than *"I'm going to sell spec to a big studio next year, fund my own festival darling, and change Hollywood once I've won my Oscar".* While we can't be certain anything set will happen, we can maximise the chances of positive things happening by doing all we can from our side.

Now, when I say "doing all we can", that's a loaded phrase that should be viewed realistically. Doing all we can means just that; it means being fair in our judgment over what we can achieve. It does not mean flogging ourselves, and it never means going above 100% of our capacity. This is a long and exhausting marathon that requires ongoing stamina. That stamina comes from keeping a sustainable pace and slowing down when needed. Some of the fruits of our labour will take years to come into harvest, and too many of us burn out and give up because we go in with too much intensity and expectation. Again, if you aren't having fun, something needs to change because you're choosing to run a marathon with a stone in your shoe and missing all the good things that are passing you by.

A big part of maintaining a healthy pace is tackling the right projects at the right time. It may sound grandiose to announce we're going to write something epic and challenging, but there's nothing impressive about delivering something sub-par or failing to deliver at all. The smart writers are the ones setting the bar at a height they know they can clear and sometimes going above and beyond as a result of their confidence. Some of my earliest story ideas are my biggest ideas, and ten years on, I still know I'm not the right writer to do them justice yet. I'm careful not to bite off more than I chew. Again, we go back to being a fair boss to ourselves; one who isn't all stick and no carrot.

Be Kind to Your Mind

Our brain is the muscle we flex the most when writing, and it's normal to become mentally worn out after a long period of intensive thinking. We must treat our most prized asset well, so it can not only consistently lift the creative weight needed to write a screenplay, but also become stronger and more capable over time. We need a brain that can punch hard with entertaining ideas, skip around emotional beats, duck around potential problems, and go the distance when it comes to finishing projects.

A particularly chaotic part of our thinking is the dreaming up of ideas. This can come to us at the strangest of times and in a flurry of inspiration that can appear to come out of nowhere. If we're not careful, our obsessing over new ideas can clog our minds as a big part of our ongoing mental processing becomes remembering and developing them. This is especially a problem when we're already trying to focus on another project. Like a computer needs both a CPU and RAM to operate efficiently, we need a process that keeps the processing flowing freely and information stored safely. My recommendation is a two-part digital process.

The first stage is to have a good notes app on your phone, preferably one that keeps information in The Cloud and syncs across all devices. This needs to be to hand at all times, even the middle of the night, so you can simply open your ideas document in your notes app and log your thoughts in as much detail as you can muster. The second stage is to have a more complicated document – I use a Scrivener project file, but it could be a Word file or even a script file – where all of those odd little notes are compiled and organised for safe-keeping. You'll find that you have concepts that you have new ideas for, sparking in your mind over a period of years, maybe even decades, and all those thoughts add up.

Done right and with regularity, you may find you are effectively developing multiple projects simultaneously while giving ideas the room they need to breathe before committing to going down a certain path.

In addition to this, there is the need to always be learning and maintaining ongoing personal development. What's critical here is understanding how we learn best. I've come to realise over the years that books work particularly well for me, as does mentoring, while I absolutely cannot pay attention in a classroom or sit through a webinar. I want to consume information at my own pace – fast – and I don't like being lectured. You may not be the same and may learn best from sitting in a class or watching a webinar, while any books you buy always remain on a shelf unread. No one way is better than another, but it's important we know what's best for us; otherwise, learning is going to be painful rather than enlightening.

Ultimately, we have to keep our minds healthy and know what they want, when they want it (much like a bodybuilder gives their muscles the nutrients they need to grow, and the time they need to heal). It's critical we have a psychological "happy place" such as listing to music, taking a long walk, or seeing friends so we can recharge and rebuild, as needed, to stay strong.

Cut Out the Toxicity and Embrace Authenticity

Screenwriter communities are sadly often dominated by the arrogant and the deluded. People with far too much time on their hands who channel all their fear and shortcomings into the criticism of others. They are typically no more confident or skilled than the next person and overcompensate for it by trying to knock others down to build themselves up. Exposing ourselves to them is like drinking poison – no good can come from it.

Every success story out there seems to have the same pattern; the writer was led to believe they didn't have what it takes until they connected with someone who appreciated their work. Alignment is everything in any creative pursuit. The famous artists of every generation weren't discovered by some collective attempt at objective scoring but instead because one or two people liked what they saw, heard, smelt, touched, or tasted, and their popularity grew from there.

We must be brave enough to stick to our guns and wait for the right person to cross our path rather than lick the boots of those who kick us down while believing that making them happy will ultimately make us happy too. It absolutely won't.

Those teams we eventually become part of have to be the right people, too. We must lean into those who mutually support us. That's not to say we should never accept our shortcomings nor neglect self-improvement, but we should remind ourselves there's a positive and negative place it can all come from. The guidance you want needs to come from the people who love what you're trying to do because only they will share your vision and care enough about your success. Those who hate your work will only ever try to paint over you and try to take ownership of your success.

Did the teams behind great movies with great friendships thrive on criticism of one another, or from belief in one another? Do great directors always work with the same great actors because their relationship is dysfunctional or because they feed off each other's energy? Sure, some have taken a very rocky path and seemingly succeeded in terms of money and glory, but we know the bitterness they feel for working with the wrong people taints it all. They all too often announce it, too.

Validation & Feedback

If breaking into screenwriting is the desert we must cross to reach our oasis, validation is the water we crave to keep us going. It is perfectly normal for human beings to desire positive comments on their efforts and feel reassured they are on the right track. I say this because there is a culture within the writing world that encourages aspiring writers to constantly beat themselves up and keep themselves down. It's almost like an ugly badge of honour for people to boast about how exhausted they are, how they desperately need to improve before they'll see any form of success, and how "tough love" is helping them improve their craft. It doesn't help that there are opinion leaders out there advising writers to be so painfully self-effacing that they actually go as far as to question positive comments as inherently bad for them. This toxic mindset is rampant within the amateur screenwriting world, but barely seems to exist within the professional world, which – from what I've experienced – is incredibly kind and encouraging.

Of course, balance is always needed, but negative comments come easy when trying to break in, sometimes completely unsolicited, so it's clear which side of the equation we need to strive for and hold dear. Confidence in yourself equals confidence on the page. Fun writing equals fun reading. A positive attitude nets positive relationships. The more we believe in ourselves, the more we will invest in ourselves by harnessing that motivation to keep practising, learning, and improving. Being a happy writer is incredibly powerful and rare to witness in a culture that sees that as weakness. Again, all we have to ask ourselves is, *"Am I good enough today?"* and that answer should be a resounding *"YES!"* We'll be good enough tomorrow, too, because our passion for our art will drive us to keep getting better all the time.

The alternative is to fester in the negativity. To fall foul of thinking that being told positive things like *"good job"* is actually damaging to our progress. There's hustling, and there's hurting, and smart writers learn to differentiate between the two.

Touching on a point made previously, the biggest problem new writers have is lacking any benefit of the doubt with the readers who judge their work and how this impacts their subjectivity. By the very nature of looking for validation as a new writer, you are going to be swimming against the tide because you are seen as just that – a new writer – and thus, people will go into your work loaded with presumptions about your talent. This phenomenon has been proven time and time again by people who have taken acclaimed work from acclaimed artists and submitted it for feedback under the guise of being an unknown. The feedback is often so negative it's damning!

Many writers insist feedback is vital to building a career and always valuable in some capacity. They believe the key to progressing is via feedback, which can often be brutal, and to grow a thick skin. I think this is some of the most damaging advice a new writer can be given, and it tends to stem from people who enjoy berating others on how they should write.

This is a worker bee mentality.

More often than not, this is a case of trying to please everybody in advance. Artists aren't worker bees, and great artists don't try to please anybody but themselves. Yes, that does sound arrogant, but personal fulfilment is so critical to our wellbeing it should never be ignored. Just because the industry often operates like a sausage factory does not mean we all have to become sausage makers. We have to constantly ask ourselves, *"Is this making me happy?"* because if it isn't, what's the point in doing it?

Again, some people would say that's selfish, but it really isn't; it's about loving our work and loving ourselves, because art that derives from passion is always the most valuable art out there. We, in fact, owe it to our audience just as much as to ourselves.

Here's the thing. The vast majority of people in the amateur world are in no position to give constructive feedback on craft. Storytelling is an incredibly complex form of art, and doing so via the medium of filmmaking is even more so. Throw the business world into the equation, and we may as well be talking about quantum physics. For many of us, the people we have access to, particularly in those early days, are no more equipped to provide feedback on the craft of screenplay writing than they are to provide feedback on the craft of cinematography, music composition, or set design.

Being an avid reader is not enough; being a prolific writer is not enough, nor is being a grad school teacher, an English major, or studio intern. Hell, working as a production company script reader isn't enough. What is enough? It's more often than not a case of relativity. We need feedback from other writers who are a step higher on the mountain; those who have trodden the same path as us who can point out where we need to find our next foothold. And what's more, that person needs to be the right person, the person that can appreciate our values and respect our destiny even if they are wildly different to theirs. If we can't find that, then there is no point in fielding the opinions and nonsense that spew from so many others.

\ A lot of cheap seats in the arena are filled with /
people who never venture onto the floor. They
just hurl mean-spirited criticisms and put-downs
from a safe distance. The problem is, when we
stop caring what people think and stop feeling
hurt by cruelty, we lose our ability to connect. But
when we're defined by what people think, we lose
the courage to be vulnerable. Therefore, we need
to be selective about the feedback we let into our
lives. For me, if you're not in the arena getting
your ass kicked, I'm not interested in your
feedback.

**Brené Brown, Rising Strong: The Reckoning.
The Rumble. The Revolution**

Beware trolls who use feedback to knock others down, question the integrity of self-titled consultants, and be cautious of paid readers. Take that energy and put it into finding actual working/credited writers and embracing what they have to say about writing itself, and apply what you like about their thinking to your process.

Bad Reader Feedback

- Is mostly or entirely subjective.
- Is written to ridicule, scold, or hurt.
- Focuses on superficial elements such as formatting and typos.
- Stems from a different political view.
- Comes from a position of angst toward writers and/or the industry.
- Comes from a person with no industry standing or validation of ability.
- Uses the opening pages to judge the script in its entirety.
- Isn't aligned with our artistic or commercial goal(s).
- Comes from a person who openly dislikes the premise, genre, and/or tone.
- Leans toward satisfying industry members rather than audience members.

Good Reader Feedback

- Puts aside personal taste.
- Motivates by pointing out the positives.
- Encourages development by making suggestions.
- Educates by explaining thinking on the craft.
- Considers production logistics and potential market appeal.
- Comes from a place of love and admiration for what we're trying to do.

The Best Feedback You'll Ever Get

There's one critic out there who we all need to satisfy us. One critic who never holds back on their true opinion, hounds us with their reasoning, and always shares our values – this is, of course, ourselves. I really feel there can never be enough value given to one's own opinion, yet we are often all too willing to second-guess ourselves in favour of complete strangers. We have to respect our inner discourse, we have to pay attention to our subconscious, because when all's said and done – be it resulting in outstanding success or painful failure – it's that voice that we will eventually have to listen to when we try to sleep at night.

My Mistakes with Happiness & Creativity

This is going to get a little dark, so take that as a trigger warning. Breaking into screenwriting nearly broke me and, in a bid to change our culture when it comes to mental health, I am very open about the issues I have faced and continue to face on a near-daily basis.

Like many, I turned to fiction writing as both an escape and a solution to some pretty big life problems. I remember the turning point well. I was 32 at the time and had been freelancing on and off in the marketing and graphic design world since I was 16. Having quit my job as the Creative Director of an agency a few years before, I'd gone it alone and had been doing very well for myself. I was earning twice as much and working half as hard – until it all fell apart fast in a cruel and unusual way.

My main client decided it was time to move on from using a one-man band and employ the services of an agency, and then my second-biggest client suffered a hostile takeover. I'd lost everything I'd built up over the years in a matter of weeks. I ran on fumes for a few months, wrapping up various tasks as any contracts expired until – while sitting at my desk alone in my home office – I stopped, stared through the computer screen into the distance, and proceeded to what I can only describe as suddenly throw up emotion through my eyes.

A complete mental breakdown is a strange thing to go through the first time, and as I fell to the floor sobbing with the cats staring down at me, I genuinely considered calling my girlfriend as I feared I was about to have a heart attack. Then, a few moments later, I lifted myself from the puddle of tears on the floor, sat back in my chair, and continued to work like nothing had happened. But something had happened. Everything had changed because, little to my knowledge, I'd become a writer and it was about to nearly destroy me.

For the record, the concept of me being a writer, no less a professional one, was nothing short of absurd at the time. I was not a good student at school, a daydreamer and class clown who went through a lot of daily bullying due to cystic acne that kept me a bit of a loner. I walked away with reasonable grades in English Literature and English Language, which my teacher told me she *"would never forgive me for"* because I didn't deserve to do that well. I went to college, dropped most of my subjects, and skipped university to go be a web designer when most people didn't know what the web was.

Computers were something I had a lot of skills in and, thanks to the advent of the spellchecker, I was able to hide an issue I didn't want to face; I had severe dyslexia, which meant I avoided writing as much as possible because even the act of typing was a frustrating struggle – writing coherently by hand was near impossible. So, instead of turning my daydreams into words, I drew. I drew like crazy. I didn't draw what was in front of me, something that really frustrated my art teacher; I drew entirely from my imagination. Drawing eventually migrated to graphic design, 3D modelling, and web design which kickstarted my career into marketing – a profession that seems to be creative on the surface but is really just engineering with crayons.

Looking back, I now realise I was actually creating stories in my childhood and trying to document them, albeit in a very inefficient and clumsy way. Many people who pivot into the creative arts later in life go through this epiphany where they suddenly connect the dots between what they are called to do now, and what they recall doing naturally as a kid. In my case, I was a born storyteller who struggled to write.

In those months between my freelance career starting to crumble and my mental breakdown, I was struggling to sleep, and my method to do so for most of my life had been to imagine various stories taking place in the form of movies. Decades of ideas were now circling in my mind, and drifting off at night was becoming more a case of trying to remember them all rather than enjoying them. I'd also been working with a couple of exciting young entrepreneurs who were forming a big part of my social life. The topic of movies had come up, and I'd revisited a book my girlfriend had gifted me during our first Christmas together, *Quentin Tarantino: Shooting from the Hip* by Wensley Clarkson, which detailed Tarantino's life up to the release of *Pulp Fiction*. On top of this, I was also volunteer-driving for the emergency services and a comment from a paramedic I drove through a snowstorm with, one night, really lodged in my mind. He'd been watching a movie when I picked him up and casually commented as we drove alone talking film that it was crazy how someone *"could just write a script one day and become a millionaire the next".*

This all became a collision of newfound free time in front of a computer, a need to get reoccurring thoughts out of my head, a refresher on how a writer broke in to make it big, and a desperate need to kickstart some kind of rewarding career. I went in positively, not realising this merging was actually a collision fit for a J. G. Ballard novel.

For the record, I have never thought you can write a script one day and become a millionaire the next. The comment narked me at the time, but it also felt like the universe was trying to give me a sign that film was the path to salvation and being able to keep paying our mortgage.

My mistake on day one was conflating my needs and expectations when it came to screenwriting. I didn't see what a potential recipe for disaster all this was, because I'd had no experience in the creative arts previously. I didn't appreciate just how hard it is to break into a screenwriting career, how much craft development and networking it takes, along with how strong a person you need to be. I was going in weak, desperate, and naive.

Like many writers in this position, the floodgates opened and I wrote like I was possessed. There was so much to get out of my system and I quickly fell in love with the act of writing itself, locking myself away at every opportunity to type and – when I wasn't doing that – I was thinking intensely about what I wanted to write. I was obsessed, falling prey to maladaptive dreaming and disconnecting from reality. Worse still, I thought I had something special. I figured turning it all into something lucrative wasn't all that far-fetched, and my daydreaming expanded to fantasies of making it big and becoming celebrated. In my head, I wasn't someone whose primary career was actually stalling and whose savings were dwindling. I was a phoenix about to rise from the ashes. It was destiny. I had three screenplays and two novels written in my first year. How hard could it be to get an agent or a book deal, right?

My friends and family were mostly very supportive and thought this was a wonderful direction for me to go in. They were just as excited as I was but couldn't see that I had checked into crazy-town long ago. My girlfriend, however, could see it all too clearly and it was upsetting to witness. She was watching the man she loved become increasingly unstable, plagued with paranoia, anxiety, and impatience. She saw my eyes turn dark and my body wither as I lacked both food and sleep. I was a ranting insomniac falling prey to clinical depression.

We didn't catch it, and deal with it there and then, because I convinced her it was all passion, and she trusted me when I argued it was all going to pay off soon. She trusted me until we hit a particularly dark day… the day after Christmas that year.

I'd fallen prey to more than demons. I'd gotten sucked into submitting my early material to a new evaluation website that ranked scripts and seemed to promise the world for those that scored well. After some good reviews earlier that month, and the need to get only a couple more to shoot up the scoreboard, I was hit with two bad ones that trashed my average numbers, my efforts, and my confidence. She could see how my face changed when I checked my email and realised what had happened. I think it was at this point she knew how vulnerable I was and how dangerous this could be.

The rest of the descent downward is a bit of a blur and an ongoing slog of pure misery that I'm perhaps blanking out now. I continued writing and tried every avenue I could to get traction, teased by moments of positivity and cut down by what felt like endless criticism. Competitions, queries, and communities. The feedback I was using for guidance was conflicting and sometimes damning. I was literally told by some that I was *"A bad writer"*. All of it was doing more harm than good, and even the blogs seem to be an indirect attack – telling me about flaws I didn't even know I might have – and demanding I stop feeling too confident and started pushing myself much harder.

Depression became suicidal ideation and my plans to end it all became ironically immortalised in my words with my characters acting them out. My work, while improving a little in terms of craft through sheer experience, became darker and even more polarising and thus a lot more prone to negative feedback. I was on a downward spiral of letting my demons take over the writing and – on the day they nearly got the better of me, the day I left my body in spirit – my girlfriend Jo, terrified by what she was witnessing and with no idea what to do, somehow managed to help me see another morning and face another day, now with a plan to address the horror that had become my determination to become a screenwriter at any cost. The dream had become a living nightmare, and it was ruining our lives.

It amazes me how far gone I was before I got help and how little warning there was out there in the screenwriting world that things could turn this way. If writing was my therapy, then surely it should have been therapeutic! Instead, it was the opposite and, if anything, I'd been encouraged to turn it into something ugly and pressured to take part in activities that were almost certainly going to leave me in pain.

I started to see this in the other artists I knew. My sister who was trying to build a unique printable crafts brand on a platform that was allowing copyright theft to run rampant. My friend who was going through the incredibly brutal world of ballet auditions because she simply wanted to be able to dance and still put food on the table. This was sadly normal in the creative arts, even sometimes seen as a rite of passage, and nobody was really talking about it. I should have spoken to them about it more because they were more experienced and much tougher than me, but I didn't because I was an older guy and, I guess, didn't want to appear weak and scared. In an ideal world, a working screenwriter would have descended magically from the sky, deus ex machina-style, to remind me that the negative opinions really meant next to nothing in a world of subjectivity, and those harshly-worded opinion pieces on craft and career-building were written almost exclusively as clickbait designed to strike fear and go viral. They would have told me the judges were nobodies, and the gurus were failing behind the scenes. What I really needed to focus on was advice from successful sources and the mechanics, along with the history, of the industry and pop culture itself.

Alas, rather than my writing helping the therapy, it was the therapy instead that ended up helping the writing. I started working on my wellbeing, finding work to earn money in the meantime, exercising, eating right, going outside, socialising, and ultimately both producing and absorbing the serotonin I'd been lacking. I'd been fearful that this would all be a huge detriment to my creativity, but it was quite the opposite. The happier and more fulfilled I became, the happier and more fulfilling my writing became with it. Sure, I was determined – very determined still and passionate with it – but I managed to migrate screenwriting into the hobby it should have been from the start, while I did something else very important… I stopped trying to naturally wing it.

Craft, or to be more specific, the academic view on craft, was something that both intimidated and irked me. I wanted to be talented, but I had mistaken what talent was. I thought it was a natural ability to perform on-demand, a genetic trait, but talent is more a case of having systematically practised something to a point where we negate any weaknesses. My weakness was mainly story structure (a pretty big one!) and I had been convincing myself that my strengths in dialogue and action scenes would make up for it. Reading my first book on craft was incredibly enlightening and helped my abstract mind comprehend aspects of story I couldn't previously see. It was also the first time a working screenwriter had "spoken" to me, so to speak, in that I felt the advice was coming from a proven place, evident in its quality, logic, and detail, compared to what I was being told by other writers online.

My writing migrated from simply creating a new blank document and ad-libbing my way through (based on some loose notes) to developing ideas, building character backgrounds, establishing themes, and forming treatments. This was powerful, but I went too deep down the rabbit hole of introspection. The process I was using wasn't free-spirited; it was highly technical and, since I wanted to turn it into a career, I was also being led into trying to write what I thought the studios wanted. This culminated in me giving up on a script for the first time. I'd bitten off way more than I could chew and created something so monstrous in its complexity and so far away from my core passion, I couldn't find the motivation to do it justice. I literally had every beat planned out, yet didn't care enough to fill them in. I'd gained knowledge and lost my spark. Precisely what I was worried might happen as a result of going into the literature on craft in the first place. My fear was that I'd killed off my talent and replaced it with procedure, like how the light-hearted drawing of my teens migrated into the cold engineering of graphic design in adulthood. This wasn't fun anymore, it was work, and worse still, speculative work that I was doing for free.

I needed a revelation, and it came to me in a strange way. My girlfriend returned home from a business trip one evening feeling a little rejected that her dinner plans with a friend had been cancelled. I took her out to one of our favourite bars to cheer her up, and we sat in the window talking about values, authenticity, happiness, and how it all applies to our careers. We couldn't get our heads around why we suffered friction working with some people while we got on so well working with others. We stumbled upon an answer; that we all tend to work predominantly for one of three things: our superiors, our craft, or our audience. Now I can't tell you how much that affected me as a writer. It was at that moment that I was able to realise that I'd become misdirected. I'd become obsessed with serving the craft and preoccupied with serving my superiors. Was I serving my audience? Well, the audience, in this case, was just *me*, and I didn't love the kind of thing I was writing. The answer was a resounding NO!

I've come to learn that, if we aren't serving our audience, those people we want to sit down and enjoy the film created from our writing, if we aren't caring as much about those people as we are about formatting, structure, presentation, and what producers want, then why are we even bothering? Serving our audience causes us to remain authentic because we should be a member of that audience, and if we can remain authentic, we will find fulfilment. That can come from simply knowing we have written something true to our heart, and if that is the case, nothing can stop us from us enjoying every word we put on paper, smiling at every line our characters speak in our heads, and feeling nothing but happiness from our writing.

What I'd stumbled upon was the importance of artistic voice, and the mistake I'd made was effectively silencing my own by trying to be highly commercial and impressing people with the sheer scale and complexity of my stories. This had caused me to fall out of love with the writing process, not because it had become procedural but because the essence of what I was working with didn't inspire me enough to carry the creation process through to the end. I was a child of the Independent Cinema Movement of the 90s with a love for the American New Wave films of the 70s. I grew up on gritty cult movies that punched above their weight and here I was… trying to pen a polished blockbuster that would appeal to modern-day teens. My mind was fighting my soul.

I knew that I needed to learn to love the process again, and I knew the key to that was learning to love myself again. I'd suppressed so much about who I was in a bid to appeal. I'd taken all that I worried was too weird and quirky and pushed it down out of embarrassment when, in fact, I should have been leaning into it and letting it flourish.

True artists do not feel shame in creating the art they feel the need to create and, the irony is, when you start writing unapologetically for yourself first and foremost, it actually pulls in the very people you felt you could never please in the first place. What I came to accept was that my place, in terms of breaking in at least, wasn't with the big studios and that moment of truth – rather than dulling my dreams – lifted a tremendous weight from my shoulders.

The reading I was doing now focused on the business of filmmaking, and the life of being an artist confirmed all this. I was taking in story after story about filmmakers, some of whom were my heroes, dealing with rejection for years and even decades without ever wavering in their vision or belief in themselves until they finally aligned with someone who appreciated them for their voice over everything else. These journeys that I thought had been quick and easy had been lengthy and difficult. These people had found it a struggle but, because they loved the work they were doing, they were unstoppable.

What I did was take the bar I was trying to leap over and not just lower it but set it on the ground. I chose to write small movies that anyone could make. Small movies I never originally thought I'd ever have the ability to write because, without huge action pieces and Hollywood production values, they demanded so much heavy lifting from the crafting of drama itself.

I started with shorts, writing the kind of pulpy little thrillers that excited me, and refined my process into something that kept me motivated and on point. Writing was fun again. I extended my efforts back into features, and it turned into a joy. I was writing the best stuff I'd ever written and loved every moment of it. I wasn't craving feedback. I wasn't rewriting due to self-doubt. There was no fear or shame in my head, and it pulled people in who wanted to work with me, motivating me further and creating an upward spiral of effort and success. I was happy, and my imagination was more vibrant than ever. I no longer felt frustrated by the lack of a career because I was so fulfilled by what I could happily keep as a hobby.

Through all this, the cult-think among amateur screenwriters online became increasingly apparent to me, and I started to see a lot of the toxic advice that I now realised had helped drive me into a very dark and self-destructive place before. An obsession with dreaming up superficial rules, an addiction to workload, a love of being servile to corporate thinking, a determination to jump through hoops, writers were constantly being told to suck up the misery and grow a thick skin. These communities actively told people to focus solely on the "business" part of show business, and I watched keen new writers enter with open minds and vibrancy only to become more cynical killjoys after being indoctrinated.

Everybody wanted to sell something to the big studios for lottery-winning sums in the easiest and most dispassionate way, by writing material that checked all the magic boxes, and then paid to play via various exposure services. I watched predatory services tempt people with gambling money for opportunities. I watched consultants stir up fear to drive up business. I watched trolls tour communities looking for excuses to trash people's work. And, of course, I watched writers, some that I knew had great talent, become exhausted through effort, lose faith in themselves through criticism, and give up on their dream through apathy. The most vulnerable were the broken ones trying to escape a reality they no longer wanted to live in, via the therapy and opportunities screenwriting could bring, and the very communities that should have provided kinship and safe harbour chewed them up, emptied their pockets, and spat them out. It turned out, for everything I had gone through, I was one of the lucky ones.

Keeping as far away as I could from amateur writing communities and refusing to get sucked into competitions, evaluation services, or any kind of rating system was the second-best thing I did for my happiness after rekindling my love for the writing process. That world was dominated by all the same people; people who had failed and turned miserable in the process, their bitterness weaponised to attack others and take them down with them. Art and subjectivity played no part in their realm because they hated the idea that they had to put their faith into something so abstract and vulnerable. They wanted to be corporate drones in a corporate system – the very antithesis to creativity, but that's where the money seemed to be.

None of it was working, though, and none of them were working writers, even if they claimed to be. I knew this because I'd now learned to do my due diligence on people before taking them at face value. Nobody could prove their dogmatic advice actually worked and, if anything, provided the living breathing evidence it didn't. I'm brutally cut-throat in the way I talk about these individuals because I have first-hand experience of where their rhetoric can send people, and some of them are highly influential because they've amassed followers in the thousands. They absolutely do not belong in the arts and are a detriment to it.

No longer craving the validation of others or interested in their *"harsh truths"*, I turned to regular blogging as a way to express my thoughts, reflections, and experiences. I put it all out there without any fear of being shouted down or picked apart for my views, and the response was wonderful and empowering. What I was saying resonated not just with other screenwriters but people in filmmaking in general, ultimately connecting me with the kind of producers and directors I wanted to get in front of and showcase my work to.

When I started getting assignments, seeing my writing turned into reality, and expanding into not only writing but also producing films, I found going back into amateur writing communities like visiting an alien world and still do this day. Everything is upside-down compared to the reality of making movies, and I feel like the 'crazy one' even though I speak from direct experience. The toxicity remains rampant, and I've come to accept that perhaps it's something endemic to writers in general – we tend to be reclusive bitter people with poor social skills and a pessimistic outlook!

What shocks me most, though, is seeing the writers I first saw ten years ago – these writers that seemed to know everything and be going places because they'd triumphed in those ranking systems that had broken me – still floundering a decade later with no change in attitude. It pains me so much that we seem to have gotten it so wrong. We have to see ourselves as artists and accept how subjective the arts are, because appreciating the chaotic nature of what we're part of actually helps bring about some sanity rather than the other way around. Knowing that nothing makes sense, and nobody knows anything, stops us from trying to make sense of it all and hoping you'll know everything. It's trying to apply too much logic to the disorder that brings about the madness.

Needless to say, breaking in did wonders for my wellbeing, bringing with it confidence, financial reward, and further opportunities. When heroes from your past tell you you're writing's *"great"* in person, it's hard to then be knocked down by even an army of online haters. Yes, surviving the industry as a working screenwriter is a whole other topic (and a whole book in itself), but the faith you gain in your ability to write entertaining stories (along with the motivation you have going into a script you know will most likely be produced) is truly remarkable. It's emotional too. While I've cried tears of happiness watching scenes shot, made dear friends on film sets, and posted status updates of my dreams becoming a reality, the most intense moment was feeling the wheels on the A380 I was a passenger on touch down on the runway of LAX late at night. That moment where I felt I had finally arrived was a magical mixture of pride, vindication, thankfulness, and humility that purged so many years of pain and frustration. All I could think about was how I wanted to go back to that writer who felt so worthless, so ugly and unwanted, only a few years ago, and tell them it was all going to be okay.

And, of course, it's the impact it all has on the people around you that reminds you of how lucky you are (while helping keep you grounded in your roots). Do I make big movies? No. Am I critically acclaimed? No. Do my friends and family act like I shoot summer blockbusters and walk red carpets? Yes! And I love them for it because they remind me how extraordinary it is to make films at any level and of any kind.

They live vicariously through my experiences, and they remind me why I turned to this when my life fell apart at the seams. My mum has squealed with joy and cheered me on from the day I started writing, and decorates the family home every time something is in production. My dad, who was hesitant to be overly encouraging at first – fearing I'd never make it against the odds – couldn't have been more proud to drive me to the airport and tell his friends where I was flying to. To bring that joy to them, along with my sister, her family, my extended family, plus my friends and all the new connections I continue to make, is a privilege and absolutely worth the struggle to make it happen.

Know this; I'm a middle-aged dyslexic with attention deficit issues and an addictive personality who's only read a few works of fiction in his life. Nonetheless, typos haven't held me back, and I've found the discipline to learn the craft and gain respect from industry members. I grew up on movies many would regard as dumb fun, and now make movies many would regard as dumb fun, yet I love what I do and have an audience that appreciates it. I was the class clown at school, and an outcast, yet I'm regarded as professional while my old classmates cheer on my successes via social media. From over 5,000 miles away and with no connections, I've managed to break into one of the most competitive industries in the world. To resort to a hacky cliché (this is our sappy ending after all), if I can do it... so can you! However, I genuinely believe that seeing yourself as an artist and loving what you do is essential to not only maintaining your wellbeing for the duration needed to break in, but also for creating genuinely entertaining, well-crafted material that stands out due to a vibrant artistic voice. So, if you are looking for permission to play, explore, indulge, and dream, then let this book be your reasoning to follow your heart and bare your soul because – right now, *more than ever* – we need more people like you adopting a positive mindset and proving that happy artists are successful artists. That message spreads around and gives those who are lost in the darkness a light at the end of the tunnel. There's your calling. Please follow it.

APPENDIX A: THE BEGINNER'S FIVE-STAGE REWRITE

So, you've written a script or maybe a few scripts and are now looking at developing your craft. You are perhaps very attached to your material, committed to marketing it, but feel it may need some work. (Spoiler alert: if you aren't sure, then it almost certainly DOES need some work).

Be proud of yourself for having the humility to accept that flaws may exist and that you are willing to learn. Many simply keep on writing and writing while waiting for their Oscar to come to them. As ever, you absolutely should be reading as many books on writing, screenwriting, art, movie history, and the business of networking as you can, but here's a quick and easy to follow guide which will help you rapidly improve your early scripts while picking up new skills along the way.

Stage 1 – Concise Writing

Cut the page count by at least 20%.

Make it a hard rule with no exceptions, but make a backup of everything you have.

If you've written a 120-page script, you must now make it 96 pages or less. Do it by cutting back your action lines to create more white space. Shorten your scenes, so you come in late and exit early. Reduce the amount of dialogue by getting to the point and using subtext. Cut out complexity by merging multiple characters into one. Trim action scenes, so they run at around one minute per page. Make your goal to get that page count down as much as possible while still having a complete story.

Stage 2 – Structure & Pacing

Take every scene and list them along with how many pages they take up. Now look at the basics of a story structure; it can be *Save the Cat*, *Turn & Burn*, or *The Hero's Journey*; it doesn't matter. Take the main acts (the number of which will vary) from that structure and determine where they intersect with your story. Add the story sections to your list as section headings with the relevant scenes under each. You now have a page count for each act, and you might find you have a lot of scenes that overfill some sections and pack little to none in others. That's okay. You now know where your script is running too long and where it's lacking. Decide on what scenes you need to cut/shorten/merge, and consider how you're going to fill in any gaps that exist with elements such as backstory, character development, and exploration of theme.

Stage 3 – Themes & Scenes

Think hard about what your story is really about – not the plot – what the story is trying to say about life and if it's proving that to be true. This is your theme.

It may be elusive.

The easiest place to find it is in your protagonist's darkest moments; times when they must face their flawed thinking and change their mindset. Now, take the scenes that you know you are going to keep and create a sub-section of notes for each one (via your screenwriting software or a spreadsheet). In these notes for each scene, identify the scene turnaround (if it has one), how it communicates the theme (if it does at all), where the conflict exists (character vs character, character vs environment, character vs inner demons), and score each scene in terms of action, humour, emotion, and tension. You now know where your scenes are performing less than optimally.

Stage 4 – Better Bad Guys

It's very easy to write a one-dimensional antagonist who's simply evil and derives pleasure from exercising that evil. Ideally, your antagonist should be a hero within their own world who has their own moral code. Ultimately, your antagonist should help communicate your theme by providing the strongest argument possible against it. An argument that is going to be proven wrong by your protagonist.

A convincing story shows both sides of the thematic debate on life and demonstrates how the more enlightened side wins. This may help you significantly in the areas where your story is lacking, and assist you on where you need to fill in those empty sections.

Stage 5 – Re-tool & Redraft

Now you know what you need to cut up and paste back together, hold back on attempting a page 1 rewrite. Adopt the scriptment approach; take your script, add in slugs for your new scenes (they can be vague locations for now), and bullet point the new beats for these scenes.

You can start with just the scene turnaround and build out from there if you want, or use the PASTO system I described earlier in this book. Add lines of dialogue that come to you. Make notes on the page. Break down old scenes you need to re-work and jiggle around those bullet points until you're happy. Now go in and write/rewrite those scenes based around those beats you've identified. Aim for 80-100 pages max.

*

Hopefully, at the end of this, you will have a much stronger script without committing to numerous painstaking rewrites that send you into development soup, while having seen a dramatic improvement in your skills via the process. Congratulations, you have the basics in place, and you can go on to learn about more detailed areas of the craft.

APPENDIX B: CRAZY CRITICS

You may have gone out there and offered your wares to the world – perhaps via a script evaluation service, competition, or coverage service – and gotten some very harsh feedback thrown back at you along with an equally disappointing score/ranking/rating.

It's easy to take critical feedback to heart, and take it as gospel, but it's essential to remember that it's only one person's opinion, and those who love to criticise sure do get it wrong a lot of the time.

> Vertigo was dismissed as corny hack work when it was released in 1958. Last year, the British Film Institute voted it the greatest film ever.
>
> **Kim Novak**

So, to help you see just how subjective this game is, here's a fun read through of responses to some of the most revered films made in the past century. Please keep in mind that these aren't the thoughts of anonymous trolls or those being paid minimum wage to churn out cheap feedback. These are responses by professional critics who actually got paid to submit their "hot takes" to respected publications. Bask in the pure cringe of their self-righteous snark, try not to die of second-hand embarrassment, and always remind yourself that your heroes never let stuff like this get to them.

The novelty wears off and the lack of imagination, visual and otherwise, turns into a drag. The Dark Knight is noisy, jumbled, and sadistic. (5/10) *The Dark Knight*, David Edelstein, New York Magazine (Vulture)

But imagination and energy are often not enough. On balance, this is the dumbest of the entries in Hollywood's anti-consumerist new wave. (5/10) *Fight Club*, Andrew O'Hehir, Salon

It is also glib, shallow, and monotonous, a movie that spends so much time sanctifying its hero that, despite his "innocence," he ends up seeming about as vulnerable as Superman. (5/10) *Forrest Gump*, Owen Gleiberman, Entertainment Weekly

There's not much humor to keep it all life-size, and by the final stretch it's become bloated, mechanical, and tiresome. (5/10) *The Matrix*, Jonathan Rosenbaum, Chicago Reader

Scorsese's style, fierce as it is, doesn't accomplish what he clearly expected of it. Often, in many arts, fresh treatment can redeem familiar subjects, but it doesn't happen here. (5/10) *Goodfellas*, Stanley Kauffmann, The New Republic

Billed as one of the most frightening, depraved films ever made. Would that it were so. Instead, this is a case of much ado about nothing. (5/10) *Silence of the Lambs*, Gene Siskel, Chicago Tribune

Nothing that suggests an independent vision, unless you count seeing more limbs blown off than usual. (5/10) *Saving Private Ryan*, Jonathan Rosenbaum, Chicago Reader

Simply a case of severe overreaching and the illusion that an overstuffed movie is an epic movie. (5/10) *The Green Mile*, Tom Keogh, Film.com

Shakespearean in tone, epic in scope, it seems more appropriate for grown-ups than for kids. If truth be told, even for adults it is downright strange. (5/10) *The Lion King*, Washington Post

What is offered instead is merely gruesome. The trail leads to a sagging, swamp-view motel and to one of the messiest, most nauseating murders ever filmed. At close range, the camera watches every twitch, gurgle, convulsion and haemorrhage in the process by which a living human becomes a corpse... The nightmare that follows is expertly gothic, but the nausea never disappears. (5/10) *Psycho*, Time

I lost track of how many times I checked my watch during the nearly three interminable hours it took Heat to play itself to a predictable conclusion of a chase scene and a shoot-out. (5/10) *Heat*, James Berardinelli, ReelViews

Inglourious Basterds is not boring, but it's ridiculous and appallingly insensitive. (5/10) *Inglourious Basterds*, David Denby, The New Yorker

On a technical level, there's a lot to be said for Die Hard. It's when we get to some of the unnecessary adornments of the script that the movie shoots itself in the foot. (5/10) *Die Hard*, Roger Ebert, Chicago Sun-Times

Begins, at two-hours-plus, is a nonstarter. (5/10) *Batman Begins*, Ken Tucker, New York Magazine (Vulture)

Speaking of jail, 'Shawshank'-the-movie seems to last about half a life sentence. The story, chiefly about the 20-year friendship between Freeman and Robbins, becomes incarcerated in its own labyrinthine sentimentality. (4/10) *The Shawshank Redemption*, Desson Thomson, Washington Post

The only remarkable thing about Francis Ford Coppola's The Godfather, Part II is the insistent manner in which it recalls how much better his original film was... Even if Part II were a lot more cohesive, revealing, and exciting than it is, it probably would have run the risk of appearing to be the self-parody it now seems. (4/10) *The Godfather Pt2*, Vincent Canby, The New York Times

Mainly it's marking time: the characters take a definite backseat to the special effects, and much of the action seems gratuitous, leading nowhere. (4/10) *Star Wars; The Empire Strikes Back*, Dave Kehr, Chicago Reader

To the degree that you will want to see this movie, it will be because of the surprise, and so I will say no more, except to say that the "solution," when it comes, solves little – unless there is really little to solve, which is also a possibility. (4/10) *The Usual Suspects*, Roger Ebert, Chicago Sun-Times

It's big, cartoonish and empty, with an interesting premise that is underdeveloped and overproduced. (4/10) *Back to the Future*, Sheila Benson, Los Angeles Times

Clearly, director Nolan is aiming for something else. But the delight in sheer gamesmanship that marked his breakout "Memento" doesn't survive this project's gimmickry and aspirations toward "Les Miserables"-style epic passion. (4/10) *The Prestige*, Dennis Harvey, Variety

The finished film remains a mess of tangled, turgid continuity and florid, mock-operatic style – at best a collection of production numbers and set pieces waiting in rain for a story capable of accumulating suspense and meaning. (4/10) *Apocalypse Now*, Gary Arnold, Washington Post

Once you've seen it all once, I bet you'll wish you were watching 'Groundhog Day' – again. (4/10) *Memento*, Marjorie Baumgarten, Austin Chronicle

The crazier Nicholson gets, the more idiotic he looks. Shelley Duvall transforms the warm sympathetic wife of the book into a simpering, semi-retarded hysteric. (4/10) *The Shining*, Variety

Van Sant's direction is surprisingly static and conventional, which doesn't help this earnest, underwhelming misfire. (4/10) *Good Will Hunting*, Keith Phipps, The A.V. Club

The only thing Mr. Tarantino spells out is the violence. I have seen much more blood spilled, yet I felt sickened by the coldness of this picture's visual cruelty. (4/10) *Reservoir Dogs,* Julie Salamon, The Wall Street Journal

If you're going to invest three hours watching a movie about a convicted stock swindler, it needs to be a whole lot more compelling than Martin Scorsese's handsome, sporadically amusing and admittedly never boring – but also bloated, redundant, vulgar, shapeless and pointles – Wolf of Wall Street. (4/10) *The Wolf of Wall Street,* Lou Lumenick, New York Post

As LaMotta, Robert De Niro gives a blank, soulless performance; there's so little of depth or urgency coming from him that he's impossible to despise, or forgive, in any but the most superficial way. (4/10) *Raging Bull,* Dave Kehr, Chicago Reader

As before, the movie is more impressive for its finely detailed vision of Los Angeles as a futuristic slum than for its story, acting, or message. It's all downhill after the first few eye-dazzling minutes. (4/10) *Blade Runner,* David Sterritt, Christian Science Monitor

All attitude and low aptitude. (4/10) *Fargo,* Richard Corliss, Time

It's obvious that Nolan either can't articulate or doesn't believe in a distinction between living feelings and dreams – and his barren Inception doesn't capture much of either. (3/10) *Inception,* Nick Pinkerton, Village Voice

Not even bags of body parts, a bitten-off tongue or a man forced to cut off a pound of his own flesh keep it from being dull. (3/10) *Se7en,* Elvis Mitchell, The New York Times

Lacks the sexy elan of 'La Femme Nikita' and suffers from infinitely worse culture shock. (3/10) *Leon: The Professional,* Janet Maslin, The New York Times

An empty-headed horror movie (1979) with nothing to recommend it beyond the disco-inspired art direction and some handsome, if gimmicky, cinematography. (3/10) *Alien,* Jonathan Rosenbaum, Chicago Reader

The surprise is that a picture made to be exciting for 136 minutes is so unexciting most of the time. It starts with a bang and keeps banging, so there's little suspense and no crescendo. (3/10) *Terminator 2: Judgement Day,* Stanley Kauffmann, The New Republic

Travels fast and straight down a linear plot, and the ceaseless rush quickly becomes monotonous. (3/10) *Indiana Jones and the Raiders of the Lost Ark,* Dave Kehr, Chicago Reader

By most standards of conventional film narrative, this movie is a mess. (3/10) *Full Metal Jacket,* Julie Salamon, Wall Street Journal

The Thing is too phony looking to be disgusting. It qualifies only as instant junk. (3/10) *The Thing,* Vincent Canby, The New York Times

Kill Bill is what's formally known as decadence and commonly known as crap... Coming out of this dazzling, whirling movie, I felt nothing – not anger, not dismay, not amusement. Nothing. (3/10) *Kill Bill: Vol. 1,* David Denby, The New Yorker

If it's all supposed to be in fun, why does it feel so much like an insult? (3/10) *The Big Lebowski,* Ken Fox, TV Guide Magazine

Promising outer-space majesty and deep-thought topics like some modern variation on Stanley Kubrick's "2001: A Space Odyssey," Interstellar instead plays like a confused mix of daringly unique space-travel footage like you've never seen and droningly familiar emotional and plot beats that you've seen all too many times before. (2.5/10) *Interstellar,* James Rocchi, The Playlist

It plays like a crude 'Godfather' parody, the sort that might amuse as a 10-minute sketch on 'Saturday Night Live,' but curdles and collapses as a 143-minute film. (2.5/10) *Scarface,* Jay Carr, Boston Globe

Perfectly passable kiddie escapism. It has a thrill or two, and a chill or three, but it has no poetry, little sense of wonder, no resonant subtext (Jungian or otherwise), no art... When it's over, it's gone. Extinct. (2.5/10) *Jurassic Park,* Jay Scott, The Globe and Mail (Toronto)

A mess of a film. (2/10) *American History X,* Village Voice

For those who care, Madonna has found her match in Guy Ritchie, whose absence of talent when it comes to the film medium is equal to her own. (2/10) *Snatch,* Amy Taubin, Village Voice

In the end the movie goes nowhere a hundred movies haven't already been and tells us nothing we don't already know. It does so with so much violent energy, however, it's like four brutal years at film school crammed into an hour and a half. (2/10) *Requiem for a Dream,* Stephen Hunter, Washington Post

Mechanical, soulless. (2/10) *Indiana Jones and the Last Crusade,* Jonathan Rosenbaum, Chicago Reader

Put simply, in my humble opinion, Oldboy sucks. (1/10) *Oldboy*, L.A. Weekly

APPENDIX C: 23 LOVE STORY TYPES

Here is the best list of love story types I have been able to put together. There may be more – I wouldn't know – I'm a bit of a crazy cat man. What's key in a lot of these is that they have an inherent dramatic conflict within them that's going to potentially work within your plot and give your characters something else to overcome.

I like to take any initial love story ideas I have in my head for a new project and run through this list to see if it sparks any further thinking.

1. Love at first sight
2. Love that complicates a personal journey
3. Love that's forbidden
4. Love found despite hate
5. Love blossoming from friendship
6. Love triangle
7. Love affair
8. Love for someone who is in disguise
9. Love for someone from a different background
10. Love complicated by baggage
11. Love complicated by distance
12. Love seemingly not reciprocated
13. Love in denial
14. Love born out of passion
15. Love that seems too sweet
16. Love for someone who is a complete opposite
17. Love for someone who is very similar
18. Love for a partner in crime
19. Love both fuelled and compromised by drama
20. Love arranged
21. Love as a new concept
22. Love that's long-term
23. Love for someone nearly lost

APPENDIX D: 147 VICES

So, your protagonist needs a major flaw that they must get over before they can see the truth and use that truth – along with a little faith –to earn their ending. Here's a list of potential options to choose from.

Try to fit a flaw to theme. For example, if the truth within your story is something like how we all need to avoid falling prey to self-destructive temptation, it might be that you demonstrate this through a character that has a history of chronic addiction issues.

Addiction – A state of physiological or psychological dependence on a potentially harmful drug.

Adultery – voluntary sexual relations between a married person and somebody other than his or her spouse.

Aggression – threatening behaviour or actions.

Alcoholism – dependence on alcohol consumption to an extent that it adversely affects social and work-related functioning and produces withdrawal symptoms when intake is stopped or greatly reduced.

Anger – a strong feeling of grievance and displeasure.

Antagonism – hostility or hatred causing opposition and ill will.

Arrogance – the act of feeling or showing self-importance and contempt or disregard for others.

Avarice – an unreasonably strong desire to obtain and keep money.

Bias – an unfair preference for, or dislike of, something.

Bigotry – when somebody with strong opinions, especially on politics, religion, or ethnicity, refuses to accept different views.

Boastfulness – to refer immodestly to possessions or achievements.

Bragging – to talk with excessive pride about an achievement or possession.

Brutality – unrelentingly harsh and severe; extremely ruthless or cruel.

Callousness – showing no concern that other people are, or might be, hurt or upset.

Chauvinism – unreasoning, overenthusiastic, or aggressive loyalty to a particular gender, group, or cause.

Cheating – to deceive or mislead somebody, especially for personal advantage.

Conceit – a high opinion of your own qualities or abilities, especially one that is not justified.

Condescension – behaviour that implies that somebody is graciously lowering himself or herself to the level of people less important or intelligent.

Corruption – dishonest exploitation of power for personal gain; extreme immorality or depravity.

Covetousness – to have a strong desire to possess something that belongs to somebody else.

Cowardice – an absence of courage.

Crabbiness – a disposition to be ill-tempered; irritable in character.

Crankiness – disagreeable and easily irritated or annoyed.

Craziness – not showing good sense or practicality; one affected by a psychiatric disorder.

Cruelty – deliberately and remorselessly causing pain or anguish; bringing about pain and distress.

Cupidity – greed, especially for money or possessions.

Decadence – a state of uninhibited immoral self-indulgence.

Deceitfulness – intentionally misleading or fraudulent.

Dementedness – completely unreasonable or lacking any sense of the consequences of actions taken; affected by the loss of intellectual functions.

Depressive – to make somebody feel very sad or hopeless.

Despairing – somebody that makes somebody else feel hopeless or exasperated; to feel there is no hope.

Discourtesy – behaviour or an action that is bad-mannered or impolite.

Dishonesty – the use of lies or deceit, or the tendency to be deceitful.

Disloyalty – a lack of loyalty to a person, vow, organization, or state.

Disrespect – total contempt; to treat another with disregard.

Doubt – to feel unconvinced or uncertain about something, or think that something is unlikely.

Egoism – the practice of making personal welfare and interests a primary or sole concern, sometimes at the expense of others.

Envy – the resentful or unhappy feeling of wanting somebody else's success, good fortune, qualities, or possessions.

Erratic – not predictable, regular, or consistent, especially in being likely to depart from expected standards at any time.

Extremism – the holding of radical political or religious views or the taking of extreme actions on the basis of those views.

Faithlessness – not believing in a religious faith; not to be trusted or relied on.

Falseness – done with, or having, the intention of deceiving somebody; treacherous.

Fanaticism – a holder of extreme or irrational enthusiasms or beliefs, especially in religion or politics.

Fearfulness – nervous and easily frightened.

Foolishness – showing, or resulting from, a lack of good sense or judgment.

Fussiness – an irritable petulant feeling; unnecessary elaborateness in details.

Glumness – quietly melancholic or miserable; gloomily ill-tempered.

Gluttony – the act or practice of eating and drinking to excess; to do anything to the point of wastefulness.

Greed – an overwhelming desire to have more of something, such as money, than is actually needed.

Grouchiness – easily upset; angry; tending to complain; habitually bad-tempered and irritable.

Grumpiness – a fussy and eccentric disposition; bad-tempered or sullen.

Hastiness – to do things or act in a hurry because of impetuosity or lack of time.

Hatred – a feeling of intense hostility towards somebody or something.

Haughtiness – behaving in a superior, condescending, or arrogant way.

Heartlessness – having or showing no pity or kindness.

Hedonism – a devotion, especially a self-indulgent one, to pleasure and happiness as a way of life.

Hubris – excessive pride or arrogance.

Hypocrite – somebody who pretends to have admirable principles, beliefs, or feelings but behaves otherwise.

Hysteria – being impossible to hold back or control; to be afflicted with a state of extreme or exaggerated emotion such as excitement or panic, especially among large numbers of people.

Idiocy – extreme lack of intelligence or foresight.

Idleness – lazy and unwilling to work.

Impatience – tending to be annoyed at being kept waiting or by being delayed; unable to tolerate a particular thing and easily annoyed by it.

Impetuosity – to act on the spur of the moment, without considering the consequences.

Inanity – meaninglessness or senselessness that suggests a lack of understanding or intelligence.

Incompetence – lacking the skills, qualities, or ability to do something properly.

Indolence – lethargic and not showing any interest or making any effort.

Infidelity – unfaithfulness or disloyalty, especially to a sexual partner.

Inflexibility – firmly established and impossible to change; adhering firmly and stubbornly to a viewpoint or principle.

Injustice – unfair or unjust treatment of somebody, or an instance of this.

Insanity – extreme foolishness, or an act that demonstrates such foolishness.

Insolence – showing a malicious or aggressive lack of deference in speech or behaviour; the quality of being boldly rude or disrespectful.

Intemperance – having or showing a lack of self-control, especially in expressing feelings or satisfying physical desires.

Irritability – easily annoyed or exasperated; extremely sensitive, especially to aggravation.

Jealousy – to feel bitter and unhappy because of another's advantages, possessions, or luck; to feel suspicious about a rival's or competitor's influence, especially in regard to a loved one.

Languor – a pleasant feeling of weariness or weakness; listlessness and indifference in speech or behaviour.

Lavishness – given or produced in abundance or to excess.

Laziness – unwilling to do any work or make an effort.

Lethargy – a state of physical slowness and mental dullness resulting from tiredness, disease, or drugs.

Lewdness – inclined to, characterized by, or inciting to lust or lechery; lascivious; obscene or indecent; salacious.

Liar – someone who does not tell the truth.

Licentiousness – pursuing desires aggressively and selfishly, unchecked by morality, especially in sexual matters.

Lunacy – behaviour that is regarded as unintelligent, inconsiderate, or misguided, or an example of it.

Lust – the strong physical desire to have sex with somebody, usually without associated feelings of love or affection.

Madness – rash or thoughtless behaviour.

Malice – the intention or desire to cause harm or pain to somebody; or to wish for someone to feel pain.

Manipulative – using clever, devious ways to control or influence somebody or something.

Melancholic – feeling or tending to feel a thoughtful or gentle sadness.

Mercilessness – very harsh in the judgment and treatment of others; showing no compassion toward somebody or something; to continue at a high level of violence or unpleasantness without pause or relief.

Moroseness – deep sadness; showing a brooding ill humour.

Moodiness – having temperamental and changeable moods; tending to change mood unpredictably from cheerful to bad-tempered.

Murderous – capable of, guilty of, or likely to commit murder.

Narcissism – excessive self-admiration and self-centeredness; overestimation of one's own appearance and abilities and an excessive need for admiration.

Obduracy – stubbornly persistent in wrongdoing; not repentant.

Obsessive – a particular action or thing that occupies one's thoughts constantly and exclusively; worrying compulsively about something or things generally.

Obstinacy – stubbornly adhering to an opinion, purpose, or course, usually with implied unreasonableness.

Offensiveness – causing anger, resentment, or moral outrage, sometimes to the point of physical repugnance.

Perversion – deviating greatly from what is accepted as right, normal, or proper, relating specifically to sexual activities considered unusual or unacceptable.

Petulance – ill-tempered or sulky in a peevish manner.

Pitilessness – showing no mercy or compassion for the suffering of others.

Pomposity – an excessive sense of self-importance, usually displayed through exaggerated seriousness or stateliness in speech and manner.

Pride – a haughty attitude shown by somebody who believes, often unjustifiably, that he or she is better than others.

Prejudice – an unfounded hatred, fear, or mistrust of a person or group, especially one of a particular religion, ethnicity, nationality, sexual preference, or social status.

Preposterousness – going very much against what is thought to be sensible or reasonable.

Pretentiousness – acting as though more important or special than is warranted, or appearing to have an unrealistically high self-image.

Profligacy – extremely extravagant or wasteful.

Promiscuity – behaviour characterized by casual and indiscriminate sexual intercourse, often with many people.

Pusillanimity – lack of courage or determination; timidity.

Rage – sudden and extreme anger.

Rashness – acting with, resulting from, or characteristic of thoughtless, impetuous behaviour.

Recklessness – marked by a lack of thought about danger or other possible undesirable consequences.

Resentfulness – annoyed or bitter about having been badly treated, or characterized by such a feeling of annoyance.

Rowdiness – a rough and noisy person who often causes disturbances.

Rudeness – disagreeable or discourteous in manner or action; offensive to accepted standards of decency.

Ruthlessness – having or showing no pity or mercy.

Secrecy – unwillingness to reveal information.

Self-importance – an unrealistically high evaluation of your own importance or worth.

Self-indulgence – lack of self-control in pursuing your own pleasure or satisfaction.

Self-pity – the self-indulgent belief that your life is harder and sadder than everyone else's.

Selfishness – concerned with your own interests, needs, and wishes while ignoring those of others.

Senselessness – apparently or really without purpose or meaning; demonstrating a lack of reason and intelligence.

Short-Sightedness – doing or determining without taking the future into account.

Sloth – a dislike of work or any kind of physical exertion.

Snobbishness – displaying an offensively superior condescending manner.

Spite – a malicious, usually small-minded, desire to harm or humiliate somebody.

Stingy – not generous in giving or spending money.

Stubbornness – unreasonably and obstructively determined to persevere or prevail.

Sulkiness – a sullen, moody, resentful disposition; in a bad mood and refusing to communicate because of resentment for a real or imagined grievance.

Sullenness – dourly disposition; showing bad temper or hostility by a refusal to talk, behave sociably, or cooperate cheerfully.

Tetchiness – oversensitive and easily upset or annoyed.

Thieving – to steal something, or steal things.

Thoughtlessness – showing a lack of planning or forethought; showing a lack of consideration for other people or for consequences.

Treasonous – one willing to betray the allegiance owed by somebody to his or her own country.

Triteness – one who overuses common phrases or conversation topics and consequently makes them lack in interest or originality.

Tricky – likely to cheat or outwit somebody.

Twisted – morally unacceptable; badly affected by unpleasant experiences or constant disappointment.

Unfaithfulness – engaging in sexual relations with somebody other than a spouse or partner; untrue to commitments, duties, beliefs, or ideals.

Unloving – not giving or reciprocating affection.

Untrustworthiness – the trait of not deserving trust or confidence.

Vainglory – excessive pride in, or boastfulness about, personal abilities or achievements.

Vanity – excessive pride, especially in personal appearance.

Vengeful – having or showing a strong desire for revenge.

Voracity – unusually eager or enthusiastic about an activity.

Wastefulness – using resources unwisely.

Weakness – lack of strength, power, or determination.

Wildness – overwhelmed by a strong emotion such as anger, grief, or desire; not tame; living or having lived in the wilderness.

Wrath – strong anger, often with a desire for revenge.

Zealousness – actively and unreservedly enthusiastic to the point of fervour.

APPENDIX E: MORAL AFFECTIONS AND PROVERBS

You can use this list to help find a life-affirming proverb that identifies the theme in your script or even choose the ones that resonate with you most and build a story around the theme it suggests. Yes, it took me a long time to compile all these. How long? Too long!

Either way, it can't hurt to have a read through them because, even outside of their practice use, many of them are deeply philosophical and, like a good story with a strong theme, just might give us the guidance we're looking for.

Right

Man attracts not by good dressing but by undressing evil thoughts. *Anonymous*

The stupid ridicule right and wrong, but a moral life is a favoured life. *Anonymous*

Wrong

A man that has lost moral sense is like a man in battle with both of his legs shot off: he has nothing to stand on. *Henry Ward Beecher*

Morality is the custom of one's country and the current feeling of one's peers. Cannibalism is moral in a cannibal country. *Samuel Butler*

Morality is the theory that every human act must be either right or wrong, and that 99% of them are wrong. *H. L. Mencken*

Too cheerful a morality is a loose morality; it is appropriate only to decadent peoples and is found only among them. *Émile Durkheim*

The spread of evil is the symptom of a vacuum. Whenever evil wins, it is only by default: by the moral failure of those who evade the fact that there can be no compromise on basic principles. *Ayn Rand*

There is nothing ... quite like the moral absolutism of the young. It's easy, as a child, to believe in good and evil, in light and dark. *Anonymous*

Morality is simply the attitude we adopt towards people we personally dislike. *Oscar Wilde*

Never challenge a fool to do wrong. *French proverb*

Telling exaggeration for attraction brings destruction. *Anonymous*

Duty

Self-reliance is the best medicine for self-confidence. *Anonymous*

Useful learning is worth even by begging. *Anonymous*

Faults are thick when love is thin. *Tamil proverb*

Friend in need is the friend indeed. *Anonymous*

Being good is more vital than just reading good. *Anonymous*

Planning the ways before action is vital, but devising the means during action is fatal. *Anonymous*

Proficiency creates efficiency. *Anonymous*

The truth is that people who pull triggers are ultimately responsible, whether they're following orders or not. An army of people making individual moral choices may be inefficient, but an army of people ignoring their morality is horrifying. *Joel Stein*

The early bird catches the worm. *English proverb*

Birds of a feather flock together. *Anonymous*

A new broom sweeps clean. *Anonymous*

If the cap fits, wear it. *Anonymous*

Don't put all your eggs in one basket. *Miguel de Cervantes*

The most beautiful things in the universe are the starry heavens above us and the feeling of duty within us. *Jeff Wheeler*

Duty is heavy as a mountain but Death is lighter than a feather. *Japanese proverb*

Duty knows no family. *Japanese proverb*

Dereliction of Duty

Morality is always the product of terror; its chains and strait-waistcoats are fashioned by those who dare not trust others, because they dare not trust themselves, to walk in liberty. *Aldous Huxley*

He falls short of his duty to both who tries to serve two masters. *Latin proverb*

I will do anything except bear the responsibility of guarding a house that has two doors. *Puerto Rican proverb*

Respect

He belongs to everybody as he is kind to anybody; but when he is not kind to everybody he does not belong to anybody. *Anonymous*

Respect is greater from a distance. *Anonymous*

The greatest evidence of demoralisation is the respect paid to wealth. *Anonymous*

Antiquity is entitled to respect. *Latin proverb*

The poor man commands respect; the beggar must always excite anger. *Napoleon*

No strength within, no respect without. *Indian proverb*

The wise must be respected, even when the advice they give is not suitable. *Indian proverb*

It is only good when the old and the young respect each other. *Chinese proverb*

Respect flies away for the one who pursues it and hunts the person who is fleeing from it. *Jewish proverb*

One of the surprising things in this world is the respect a worthless man has for himself. *EW Howe*

The best thing to give to your enemy is forgiveness; to an opponent, tolerance; to a friend, your heart; to your child, a good example; to a father, deference; to your mother, conduct that will make her proud of you; to yourself, respect; to all men, charity. *Benjamin Franklin*

Never take a person's dignity: it is worth everything to them, and nothing to you. *Frank Barron*

Respect cannot be learned, purchased or acquired – it can only be earned. *Anonymous*

The devil's most devilish when respectable. *Elizabeth Barrett Browning*

Disrespect

Ignoring a child's disrespect is the surest guarantee that it will continue. *Fred G. Gosman*

Disrespect cannot be commanded, it must be earned. *Matthew Taberner*

Never make excuses for someone who disrespects you – who they are or what they do isn't a pass to treat you like trash! *Trent Shelton*

Discourtesy does not spring merely from one bad quality, but from several – from foolish vanity, from ignorance of what is due to others, from indolence, from stupidity, from distraction of thought, from contempt of others, from jealousy. *Jean de la Bruyere*

Rudeness is the weak man's imitation of strength. *Eric Hoffer*

Straightforwardness, without the rules of propriety, becomes rudeness. *Confucius*

The way to avoid the imputation of impudence is not to be ashamed of what we do, but never to do what we ought to be ashamed of. *Cicero*

Mistaking insolence for freedom has always been the hallmark of the slave. *Wilhelm Reich*

The insolence of wealth will creep out. *Samuel Johnson*

Contempt

Envy makes one's virtue empty, and empathy makes the virtue entity. *Anonymous*

None has grown richer by envying and no one has lost anything by not envying. *Anonymous*

Anger bequeaths bitter results, but its control brings better results. *Anonymous*

Let bygones be bygones. *Anonymous*

The only cure for contempt is counter-contempt. *H. L. Mencken*

Contempt for happiness is usually contempt for other people's happiness, and is an elegant disguise for hatred of the human race. *Bertrand Russell*

Of all afflictions, the worst is self-contempt. *Berthold Auerbach*

Approbation

Ever receive a present with approbation. *Anonymous*

A beaten track is a safe one. *Latin proverb*

Judge of the daughter by the mother. *Anonymous*

Disapprobation

Never judge by appearances. *Anonymous*

Flattery

He that loves to be flattered is worthy of the flatterer. *William Shakespeare*

A fool flatters himself, a wise man flatters the fool. *Edward G. Bulwer-Lytton*

Imitation is the sincerest form of flattery. *Oscar Wilde*

Detraction

Telling ill of others means tilling your own grave. *Anonymous*

Listening about others' weakness exposes one's own weakness. *Anonymous*

Flatterer

He that flatters you more than you desire either has deceived you or wishes to deceive. *Italian proverb*

Many lick before they bite. *Anonymous*

A flatterer is one who says things to your face that he wouldn't say behind your back. *Anonymous*

Accusation

A false accusation is as deadly as a sword, a club, or a sharp arrow. *Proverbs 25:18, Good News Bible*

It is an honourable thing to be accused by those who are open to accusation. *Latin proverb*

Even doubtful accusations leave a stain behind them. *Thomas Fuller*

He declares himself guilty who justifies himself before accusation. *English proverb*

A clear conscience fears no accusation. *African proverb*

Even after the accusation or rumour has been refuted, a suspicion nonetheless lingers. *Swedish proverb*

Probity

Perfect conscious will never create imperfect thoughts. *Anonymous*

Knave

Telling as if truth which is not true makes one's life false. *Anonymous*

When thieves fall out, their knaveries come to light. *Portuguese proverb*

The bad man always suspects knavery. *Spanish proverb*

Disinterestedness

Laziness is the best medicine to lose opportunities. *Anonymous*

Uneducated in high society is inferior to educated in low society. *Anonymous*

If the blind lead the blind, both shall fall. *Matthew 15:14, King James Version*

There are none so blind as those who will not see. *John Heywood*

Make hay while the sun shines. *Anonymous*

The road to hell is paved with good intentions. *Anonymous*

Easily grasped are the crimes of a hog. *Icelandic proverb*

Selfishness

Unused wealth is a liability to society. *Anonymous*

Noble men serve when in need, but mean men serve only when crushed indeed. *Anonymous*

Power with selfishness creates egoism; power less selfishness creates respect; powerless selfishness creates meanness. *Anonymous*

I think it's a problem that people are considered immoral if they're not religious. That's just not true…. If you do something for a religious reason, you do it because you'll be rewarded in an afterlife or in this world. That's not quite as good as something you do for purely generous reasons. *Lisa Randall*

Virtue

Virtuous life brings honour and neglect of it brings disgrace. *Tamil proverb*

Virtuous knows the utility of his wealth to devoid others' poverty. *Anonymous*

Be not ashamed of mistakes and thus make them crimes. *Confucius*

Poverty is not a crime, but it's better not to show it. *Brazilian proverb*

Laws control the lesser man. Right conduct controls the greater one. *Mark Twain*

A clear conscience is the greatest armour. *Anonymous*

With virtue you can't be entirely poor; without virtue you can't really be rich. *Chinese proverb*

For a righteous man falls seven times, and rises again. *Proverb 24:16*

Every virtue is but halfway between two vices. *Latin proverb*

Vice

Detachment to duties for attachment to lust paves for derailment of life. *Anonymous*

Gambling gambles with one who gambles. *Anonymous*

All that glitters is not gold. *Anonymous*

The grass is always greener on the other side. *Anonymous*

Commit a sin twice and it will not seem a crime. *Jewish proverb*

No one ever suddenly reached the height of vice. *Anonymous*

It is easier to run from virtue to vice, than from vice to virtue. *Latin proverb*

Vices creep into our hearts under the name of virtue. *Latin proverb*

Vice is nourished by concealment. *Latin proverb*

Innocence

Once you start asking questions, innocence is gone. *Mary Astor*

The innocent and the beautiful have no enemy but time. *William Butler Yeats*

A mind conscious of innocence laughs at the lies of rumour. *Latin proverb*

Innocence itself sometimes hath need of a mask. *Polish proverb*

Innocence can be an offence. *African proverb*

Guilt

There's a black sheep in every family. *Anonymous*

He who is guilty believes that all men speak ill of him. *Italian proverb*

A mind conscious of guilt is its own accuser. *Latin proverb*

Guilt is perhaps the most painful companion of death. *Elisabeth Kubler-Ross*

Good Man

Earning wealth with morality and sharing the wealth with needy keeps one's generations happy. *Anonymous*

Bad Man

Honesty is the best policy. *Anonymous*

Penitence

Peace and patience, and death with penitence. *Spanish proverb*

Impenitence

Blaming spoils relationship but suggestion builds relationship. *Anonymous*

Temperance

Control over temptation gets morality, and control over desire gets spirituality. *Anonymous*

Beware of Greeks bearing gifts. *Anonymous*

Intemperance

Two blacks don't make a white. *Anonymous*

Forbidden fruit is the sweetest. *Anonymous*

Gambling with temptation takes his family to starvation. *Anonymous*

Sensualist

Lust is allowed with license. *Anonymous*

Gluttony

Slaughtering is created by eating it. *Anonymous*

The greatest evidence of demoralisation is the respect paid to wealth. *Anonymous*

The stingy has a big porch and little morality. *Arabic proverb*

It's easy enough to preach morality on a full belly. *Erwin Sylvanus*

Beggars can't be choosers. *Anonymous*

The eye is bigger than the belly. *Anonymous*

Give a man enough rope and he'll hang himself. *American proverb*

Impurity

Saving a life is better than fasting for God. *Anonymous*

Legality

Justice is exercised in the proper prevention, rather than in the severe punishment, of crime. *Latin proverb*

Illegality

Crime leaves a trail like a water beetle; like a snail, it leaves its silver track; like a horse-mango, it leaves its smell. *African proverb*

If you share your friend's crime, you make it your own. *Latin proverb*

In times of trouble, leniency becomes crime. *Anonymous*

Crimes may be secret, yet not secure. *Italian proverb*

It's no crime to steal from a thief. *Dutch proverb*

We carry our neighbours' failings in sight; we throw our own crimes over our shoulders. *Romanian proverb*

Death is nothing and pain is nothing, but cowardice is crime and disgrace, the greatest punishment. *American proverb*

A newly committed crime awakens sleeping ones. *African proverb*

The greatest crime in a desert is to find water and keep silent about it. *African proverb*

Crime does not pay... as well as politics. *Alfred Newman*

Judge

Desperate diseases demand desperate remedies. *Anonymous*

Love me, love my dog. *Saint Bernard of Clairvaux*

Crime is cunning; it puts an angel in front of every devil. *German proverb*

The act itself does not constitute a crime, unless the intent be criminal. *Latin proverb*

Acquittal

Men's mistakes are tolerated by gentlemen. *Anonymous*

Condemnation

The crime accuses itself. *Mexican proverb*

Punishment

As you make your bed, so you must lie in it. *Anonymous*

It is the crime that causes the shame, and not the punishment. *Swedish proverb*

Criminals are punished, that others may be amended. *Italian proverb*

Punishment awaits crime. *Latin proverb*

A crime eats its own child. *African proverb*

Reward

You scratch my back, I'll scratch yours. *Anonymous*

Success consecrates the foulest crimes. *Russian proverbs*

Behind every great fortune there is a crime. *Balzac*

Scourge

The greater the man, the greater the crime. *Anonymous*

APPENDIX F: FURTHER READING

There are countless screenwriter booklists out there and, from what I've seen, a lot of them aren't even compiled by screenwriters themselves. They are pretty dire and tend to trot out the same tired pieces of literature. I've been cutting my own path with reading for a while now, and I want to share the books that I've personally learned a lot from and which have worked for me. This is what I believe is the most powerful collection of screenwriting books you can read over the next 12 months.

This list is also about the bigger picture than screenwriting itself; it covers the areas of writing, artistry, and industry, for which I've picked my favourites within each. It's important you understand film history, know what a career in the business looks like, and respect the medium as an art form.

Personally, I feel this is essential reading. I see so much ignorance within screenwriting communities over the reality behind how famous films were developed, how popular screenwriters built careers, and even what advice various authors give. That's before even getting into discussion over craft!

There's a wealth of information here you can arm yourself with. Information that will give you craft tips, creative direction, business advice, and historical knowledge that will benefit you not only in terms of your writing but your ability to network, collaborate with other filmmakers, and build a career.

None of these books are a one-shot solution. You have to take a little from each and be prepared to throw some advice away if it doesn't align with your needs. A lot of people read one book and become tribalistic over it, arguing points to death because they don't want to sit down and take in new information. That's just cutting off your nose to spite your face in the long run.

Some obvious, well-known books I'm not going to bother listing. By all means read *Save The Cat* if you want to know what it covers, and be able to discuss it with understanding should the topic come up.

Screenwriting

If you look these authors up, you may be disappointed by the lack of IMDB credits, but that doesn't invalidate them or what they have to say. Some people are just very good at analysing things. That said, there's stuff in each book that contradicts itself or is, in my opinion, just plain wrong. There's still a lot of gold within all of them, though. Just take it all as a theory along with suggestions with nothing carved in stone.

The intention here is to take the bits that work for you; subsequently, you take in the arguments behind certain points. You may also find a concept that you can't get your head around in one book becomes easy to grasp when explained in another.

Writing For Emotional Impact, by Karl Iglesias

Writing Screenplays That Sell, by Michael Hauge

Screenplay: The Foundations of Screenwriting, by Syd Field

Your Screenplay Sucks: 100 Ways to Make It Great, by William M. Akers

Story, by Robert McKee

Artistry & Creativity

A topic seldom discussed, but essential to the development of writers, is artistry. As screenwriters, we go through a lot of emotional stuff alone and the attitude within a lot of communities discredits the artistic side of our art form.

When you read these books, a lot of feelings you thought you struggled with – alone – will make an appearance. You will learn ways to fight your inner demons and get the most from yourself. Ultimately, the learning in here should help you build yourself into a happy, fulfilled artist who loves the process of creating.

Art & Fear, by David Bayles & Ted Orland

On Writing, by Stephen King

Steal Like An Artist, by Austin Kleon

Creativity, Inc., by Ed Catmull

Real Artists Don't Starve, by Thomas Nelson

The Gift: How the Creative Spirit Transforms the World, by Lewis Hyde

Industry

How would you feel if you found out that every great film you know of was hated at some point? That what's regarded as the best screenplay ever written was rejected by the film's director? How the people behind some of the most highly rated films in history had no faith in them? That some of the greatest screenwriters in history found themselves unwanted and ridiculed when they first approached Hollywood?

Legendary films have struggled to get made since filmmaking started, and the industry has always been rife with drama. The deals that have been done, the tricks that have been pulled, and the gambles that have been made are stories you really need to read about.

What You Don't Learn In Film School, by Shane Stanley

How I Made A Hundred Movies In Hollywood And Never Lost A Dime, by Roger Corman

Easy Riders, Raging Bulls, by Peter Biskind

Down and Dirty Pictures, by Peter Biskind

Rebels on the Backlot, by Sharon Waxman

Adventures in the B Movie Trade, by Brian Trenchard-Smith

Tales From Development Hell, by David Hughes

Tales from the Script: 50 Hollywood Screenwriters Share Their Stories, by Peter Hanson and Paul Robert Herman

Quentin Tarantino: Shooting from the Hip, by Wensley Clarkson

Powerhouse: The Untold Story of Hollywood's Creative Artists Agency, by James Andrew Miller

Sleepless in Hollywood: Tales from the New Abnormal in the Movie Business, by Lynda Obst

Write From The Start: The Beginner's Guide to Writing Professional Non-Fiction by Caroline Foster

Write From The Start is a book that's aimed at novice writers, hobbyist writers, or those considering a full-time writing career, and offers a comprehensive guide to help them plan, prepare, and professionally submit their non-fiction work.

It is designed to get people up-and-running fast.

Write From The Start teaches how to explore topic areas methodically, tailor content for different audiences, and create compelling copy.

It will teach readers which writing styles work best for specific publications, how to improve one's chances of securing both commissioned and uncommissioned work, how to build a portfolio that gets results, and how to take that book idea all the way to publication.

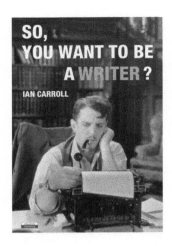

So, You Want to be a Writer? by Ian Carroll

Ian Carroll is an author of both fiction and non-fiction. Having written books that were published, self-published, and some of which never even left his desk drawer, Ian has fully experienced the writer's journey, and he now wishes to share it with new writers.

Aside from books, he has also written plays – both originals and adaptations – that have been performed at some of the biggest theatres in the UK, as well as writing screenplays for the big screen. Join Ian as he details his 30-year writing career and the lessons he has learned along the way.

This book contains advice and encouragement, helpful tips and commentary, about what it is to be – and to want to be – a writer.

So, You Want to be a Writer covers a wide range of topics and discusses different genres, formats for writing, how to overcome obstacles, and explores the many avenues that will hopefully lead you to success. Short, succinct chapters cover areas such as: How to get a Publisher; Copyright; Self-Publishing; Adapting Books; Writing Fiction and Non-Fiction; Agents; and much more.

We are not writers unless we sit down and write, and this book offers all the support you need.

So, you want to be a writer? Let's do it!

Ingram Content Group UK Ltd.
Milton Keynes UK
UKHW012012170423
420323UK00004B/26